MW01025522

DISCIPLESHIP FOR THE FUTURE

DISCIPLESHIP
FOR THE
FUTURE

SPIRITUALITY OF THE KINGDOM

FRANK P. DESIANO, CSP

Paulist Press
New York / Mahwah, NJ

Scripture quotations are taken from the New American Bible. revised edition © 2010, 1991, 1986, 1970 by the Confraternity of Christian Doctrine. Inc.. Washington, DC. All rights reserved. Used with permission.

Cover image by Alkestida/Shutterstock.com
Cover design by Joe Gallagher
Book design by Lynn Else

Copyright © 2022 by Frank P. DeSiano. CSP

All rights reserved. No part of this publication may be reproduced. stored in a retrieval system, or transmitted in any form or by any means. electronic, mechanical, photocopying, recording, scanning. or otherwise. without either the prior written permission of the Publisher, or authorization through payment of the appropriate per-copy fee to the Copyright Clearance Center, Inc.. www .copyright.com. Requests to the Publisher for permission should be addressed to the Permissions Department. Paulist Press. permissions@paulistpress.com.

Library of Congress Cataloging-in-Publication Data
Names: DeSiano, Frank P., author.
Title: Discipleship for the future : spirituality of the kingdom / Frank P. DeSiano, CSP.
Description: New York / Mahwah, NJ : Paulist Press, [2022] | Summary: "Fr. Frank DeSiano guides the reader through meditations on the power and importance of the kingdom of God and our role as we are drawn to it as disciples in hope of the future. made possible by the coming of Christ and the gift of the Spirit"—Provided by publisher.
Identifiers: LCCN 2021032020 (print) | LCCN 2021032021 (ebook) | ISBN 9780809155880 (paperback) | ISBN 9781587689918 (ebook)
Subjects: LCSH: Kingdom of God—Meditations.
Classification: LCC BT94 .D47 2022 (print) | LCC BT94 (ebook) | DDC 231.7/2—dc23
LC record available at https://lccn.loc.gov/2021032020
LC ebook record available at https://lccn.loc.gov/2021032021

ISBN 978-0-8091-5588-0 (paperback)
ISBN 978-1-58768-991-8 (e-book)

Published by Paulist Press
997 Macarthur Boulevard
Mahwah, New Jersey 07430
www.paulistpress.com

Printed and bound in the
United States of America

CONTENTS

PREFACE

FOR A LONG TIME, the importance of the Kingdom of God has been growing on me.

As I have matured in my years as a priest, and particularly as a preacher, the overwhelming importance of the Kingdom has become unavoidable. After all, what did Jesus live for, die for, rise for, and promise to return for? Of course, the Kingdom.

The power of this image of the Kingdom, mysteriously present but pregnant with a future we can barely imagine, has dovetailed in recent decades with Christian reflection on evolution, at least for those Christians who do not reject the idea of evolution because of their fundamentalist assumptions. Evolution has permitted a new perspective for human thinking, one in which, through a process of greater complexification, new forms of life emerge, indeed even the unique form of life we call humankind.

Many Christian thinkers have come to see evolution as a pattern of ongoing progress, one begun in God, drawn forward by God, and culminating in an encounter with the fullness of God. Such a perspective allows believers to look on our world optimistically, as an instrument of God's loving providence. If the Middle Ages could arrive at an idea like "the Great Chain of Being," modern people, because of evolution, can think about "the Great Chain of Becoming."

People began to intuit this new vision of hope over one hundred years ago. Henri Bergson, a French philosopher, published a book entitled *Creative Evolution* (1907) and tried to describe human reality as action. A Jesuit, Pierre Teilhard de Chardin (†1955), produced stunning books that directed humankind toward an ever-fuller future. The philosopher Alfred North Whitehead (†1947) elaborated, under the influence of the discoveries of particle physics, a philosophy of process, one that various theologians have built upon. Another Jesuit, Bernard Lonergan (†1984), said that humankind could not be understood apart from a horizon that drew human thinking and behavior forward.

Christian believers can look, then, on human experience as an ever-greater opening to a fullness latent in all human longing, but now unveiled and made operative by the coming of Jesus Christ and the sending of the Holy Spirit—God's great sending and outpouring that moves creation toward a completion that is identical with the Kingdom of God.

Christian spirituality may contain aspects of looking *back*, and it must contain aspects of looking *around* in reflection, but its fundamental orientation is looking *forward*, toward a tomorrow glimpsed only by hope. This book of reflections intends to serve just this vision etched into the Christian imagination by the virtue of hope, that power of transformed imagination bestowed by the Spirit that brings transformation to our imaginative visions and, as a result, to our lives.

If more Christians, and particularly Catholics, come to understand their lives as focused on this forward thrust of creation toward a Kingdom, and set their Christian lives in service to the promises of the Kingdom, then a better proportion can emerge in terms of the emphases of Christian action. Christian history reveals a lot of dead ends, not least of which are false triumphalism and colored-over bias. Maybe if we turn our eyes toward a future that God wants us all to own, instead of the pieces of turf we have settled for, some of the energy of Jesus's ministry will emerge more clearly once again.

My modest hope is that the following chapters will serve this purpose.

Chapter 1

SPIRITUALITY AND THE FUTURE

THOSE DECEMBER SUNDAY nights back in the 1950s must have been as dark as I remember them. They must have been cold, but the frigid air has not lingered in my memory. Rather, what lingers are memories of how, on Sunday evenings, we children would run to our five-story school building on West 60th Street in Manhattan, gathering with many of our classmates for Advent events, which got us very excited.

On the front of our church building, on what was then a large empty space waiting to be eventually filled with a bas-relief sculpture, hung a wreath at least fifty feet in diameter. Four large candles were attached, one for each week of Advent. When the signal came to each classroom, we children went down the stairs forming a procession that eventually stretched half a city block. St. Paul the Apostle School had over twelve hundred pupils; not all of them attended these pre-Christmas devotions. But enough did to fill 60th Street and the block in front of the church.

Fr. John Carvlin, our Paulist pastor, had designed this devotion. He could never be without a smile. I had the privilege of working with him twenty years later when I began serving as a Paulist priest in Portland, Oregon. He

1

still radiated joy, lifting spirits and helping even the glum to smile. Back in grade school I benefitted from Fr. Carvlin's sense of drama and joy.

"O come, O come, Emmanuel," we sang. Verse by verse this chant accompanied our procession toward Columbus Avenue. The lucky ones could squeeze in front of the church for the best view. Fr. Carvlin stood on a porch-like area at the top of the steps that led to the massive front door of St. Paul the Apostle Church. "Rejoice, rejoice, O Israel; to thee shall come Emmanuel." As the verses died down, he led us in prayers and then, with a master stroke of his hand, seemed to instruct one of the candles, wired with light bulbs, to turn on. It all seemed like magic to us.

In the darkness, we children saw the candle electrically ignite. "Wow," the hundreds of children, and their parents, whispered with a low-pitched roar. Filled with the excitement of Christmas, of our toys and friends—we could hardly wait!—each candle seemed a further step into a future that would never come soon enough. The third candle, pink and not purple in color, told us that "Gaudete Sunday" had come: "Rejoice"—not only because our salvation was drawing near, as the Latin liturgy was saying, but mostly because our long wait for Christmas morning, with its gifts, was almost over.

What doll might my sister get? Or maybe a record to play? Perhaps a baseball glove or hockey stick for my brother? Or maybe a board game? Or a new wallet? When would the cousins come on Christmas day? We had to show off our presents while piles of pasta and meat came from our tiny stove.

The dark December nights took on a glow when we had something to look forward to.

~ • ~

It is so natural to think of the future much like we children thought about Christmas those decades ago. Our state of life was Advent, the period of drawn-out time; another state was Christmas, which would come as a reward for those who deserved it. The future can seem so far away it could appear as something entirely separate from our waiting. The way we separate the present from the future works similarly to the many other separations, splits, we create when we think of lives.

Present and future. Time and eternal. This life and next life. Work and leisure. Duty and desire. Culture and religion. We want to split our experience into different aspects; then we want to divide those splits even further. The Greek philosopher Plato gave us an image we cannot erase. What if all our experience, everything that seems real, is ultimately only a copy, only derivative. What if we actually were living in a cave but didn't know that? What if the only real things were eternal and everything else just an appearance, almost an illusion?

This little parable of Plato forces us to wonder, to question everything our senses tell us. This natural world, what can it be? Beautiful, at times, but kissed by doom. Where is that other world, the eternal, the timeless? How do we enter into that? Can we do it only through dying? What do we make of the moments that we have? Are they points of endurance until the real payoff?

So we make these splits, these separations, and define our lives in terms of darkness and light, death and life, the now and the hereafter. We try to peel experience apart, analyze it into bits, define it into opposing camps. So long as we live in this split-apart universe, the future has to seem strange. The time we spend tending toward the future looks just like something to endure. According to this vision, the future does not emerge from our days. Indeed, it's on the other side of what we can experience.

But maybe, ultimately, there are not splits, oppositions, foes bound by conflict. What if experience ultimately is one, a layered reality enmeshed around itself, this dynamic thrusting that our theory of evolution tries to describe, or geologists try to draw, or biologists try to depict, or philosophers try to theorize, or faith attempts to glimpse? Maybe we can come to see layers, all penetrating each other, all interchanging with each other, all pulling us toward a cohesive vision of ourselves, our meaning, and our destiny.

What if mind is a dimension of body, and body the condition for mind? What if God designs matter so that spirit evolves from it, emerges from its seeming denseness? What if nature cannot be understood apart from the ultimate mystery from which it came and toward which it points? What if the supernatural is really a way of describing the layers of nature itself? What if moments all emerge from the timeless, and the timeless helps the moments go by? What if every work was begotten of grace, and grace's purpose was to charge every good work we tried to do?

Spirituality

As we think about a spirituality for tomorrow, I hope we can move away from some of the traditional split categories we have used to think about our lives. A big one has been this life and the next life. Others have been nature and grace, reason and faith, natural and supernatural.

Certainly, one of the clear senses of modern life has been to see our human existence as integral, as whole,

4

as one reality. One professor put it this way: "Isn't it all about experience?" He was saying that, ultimately, we only have our experience to form the basis of our awareness of ourselves and our world. Isn't that the starting place for everything? The various categories we use basically carve up our one, whole, experience of life.

Not that our experience is anywhere near complete; certainly not. It takes a minute to realize just how much of life we actually do miss, as our meditation at the end of this chapter will show. Nor is our experience isolated. In fact, our experience readily includes what we experience of others, particularly those we love and those with whom we intensively interact. We all remember one famous line from philosophy, René Descartes's phrase: "I think, therefore I am." But who really thinks all by himself or herself? We think, we talk with others, we question what we think, we talk a little more, we come to decisions. Our experience is not total nor isolated. In fact, it's an experience of great connectedness. Much of what we propose for a "spirituality toward tomorrow" revolves around the ways we are connected, and can connect, with each other and with the future.

Spirituality is a word that has always made me suspicious. It has always struck me as a kind of abstraction, a fancy word that pulls away from life's actual events to make up some theory. After all, the reality is that people do "spiritual" things like pray, help others, read sacred texts, worship. Isn't that what we are really referring to? Why invent a multisyllable word like *spirituality* that doesn't really add much to the reality?

But as I've thought about this, the word *spirituality* in the end does appear useful. It allows us, for example, to differentiate a Buddhist from a Lutheran, and a Lutheran from a Catholic. Spirituality simply refers to the assumptions, attitudes, and behaviors associated with a certain vision of life and, more particularly, a vision of a life connected with some reality like God. A Jewish man reciting prayers in Hebrew on an airplane, bowing at regular intervals, has a vision of himself and God that differs from that of a cloistered nun preparing to be part of the Eucharist. His vision of God imposes obligations on him that differ from the nun's vision of God. Indeed, even if someone thinks there is no God but still upholds ultimate values that influence behaviors, a spirituality is implicitly present.

So where would a spirituality for tomorrow come from? What would be its assumptions, attitudes, and behaviors?

How about the Kingdom of God?

All in All

In his first letter to the Thessalonians, St. Paul takes up a question undoubtedly put to him: If Christian life is about eternal life, what about our brothers and sisters, Christians, who have already died? How is it eternal life when we still have to mourn and bury those we love? (1 Thess 4:13–18). This, in a way, takes up the same question raised in John's Gospel, in the chapter when Jesus raises Lazarus from the dead. Jesus says to Martha, "Everyone who lives and believes in me will never die. Do you believe this?" (John 11:26). What does the experience of Jesus say about the relationship of "now" and "then," of "here" and "future," of "life" and "death"?

In another letter, 1 Corinthians, Paul points to a final state of risen life. This state comprises an astonishing integration of experience; Paul would never be content to think of heaven as angel-like souls sitting on clouds perfectly content with their seeming transparency. Slow as it was to emerge in Jewish thinking, the idea of the resurrection had come into its own as a dominant thought before Jesus's time; most Jews accepted the idea.

Look at how Paul sketches a vision of space and time.

> For just as in Adam all die, so too in Christ shall all be brought to life, but each one in proper order: Christ the firstfruits; then, at his coming, those who belong to Christ; then comes the end, when he hands over the kingdom to his God and Father, when he has destroyed every sovereignty and every authority and power. For he must reign until he has put all his enemies under his feet. The last enemy to be destroyed is death. (1 Cor 15:22–26)

Jesus's principal work, as Paul puts it, seems to be integrating everything into one by destroying those things that lead to human disintegration, especially, in the end, death itself. So if the final vision is the overcoming of those things that lead to dissolution, then the goal is integration of all those things that lead to the fullness of life. So complete, in fact, is the life that Jesus promises and brings about that, in the end, everything is ordered to Jesus who, in turn, orders everything to God and, in Paul's striking phrase, God is "all [things] in all" (1 Cor 15:28). The integration of experience overcomes even the gulf we erect between the divine and the nondivine. All things eventually exist in God just as God exists in all.

Although Paul conceives of this in terms of space because he talks of meeting Jesus in the clouds in another of his letters (1 Thess 4:17), one can also conceive of Paul's vision in terms of time. What Paul speaks about can be conceived as a fullness pushing through time, not necessarily "above" but "ahead"—"into the future." Or to be plainer,

7

what ancients conceived as "up" and "down," we can conceive as "then" and "now." Further, we can conceive "then" and "now" not in opposition to each other but in continuity. This is what the notion of evolution has to offer us modern people, something the ancients could not envision. We can think of time and fulfillment in continuity, as part of a single experience that integrates all the layers of our existence.

One task of spirituality is to cultivate exactly this forward thrust-toward-fullness as the vision out of which we live. If Christ is raised from the dead, then we have a glimpse of the "end times"—what fulfilled life looks like and, even more, a sign of its actualization in our midst. Christ's resurrection reveals how the layers of our existence come together through a divine love that pulls all of creation forward toward an ever-fuller future. On Easter morning the future of existence began to be revealed, began to emerge from within time.

This contrasts with the image of spiritual life that has dominated so much of Christian history. In that image, the Kingdom was an "afterlife" that came as a reward for not being bad or, in some Christian circles, for having a trusting faith. Rather than a continuity between the forward thrust of creation and its fulfillment, the image was more of a static present life in which the world, without dynamism, came to an apocalyptic end. Only then would the Kingdom be revealed. Or, if there was a dynamism in the world, this could be as likely conceived as a demonic force bending history toward greater chaos and evil, in perpetual conflict with the good.

With this perspective, being a good Christian meant keeping one's "soul" from sin, renouncing the things of the body and the world, and hoping for the chance to escape the fires of hell. Of course, countless Christians and recognized saints made much more of their Christian existence than this dour picture, as their actions flowered in prayer, service to others, and profound human needs. But the old catechisms taught us well the purpose of our lives: to know, love, and serve God in this life so that we could be with God in the next.

This also meant that spiritual life implicitly revolved around the past. What were we going to do with Adam and Eve, with Moses's Ten Commandments, with the inevitable sins that seem to mark history, whether personal or cultural? What could we do about the killing of the one who is our Messiah, seeing his bloodied body hanging on the cross? How could we go back and repair history or, for that matter, repair our own pasts? Spiritual life was more a looking backward with anxiety than looking forward with anticipation. Christian life could seem as the "reparation" of a hopelessly distorted past.

When I think back on how faith was so often put in the past, I do feel that much of Christian life was perceived under the assumed de facto absence of God. Sure, God was everywhere, but so was the devil, and so was sin, and so was the frantic sense of being outside the state of grace, a state that always felt frail and elusive. For centuries receiving holy communion was the exception, done twice a year, as we would beat on our breasts and utter, "O Lord, I am not worthy." In this kind of framework, grace seemed an elusive dazzle of light, a moment's experience right after going to confession and making a "good holy communion." So our Christian lives felt as if God were distant—with only flickers of union with God now and then. Rather than seeing ourselves progressing to the fullness of life, we trembled in fear, hoping that we might somehow sneak into a corner of purgatory where, after centuries of burning, we might make it to heaven.

An "absent" God might well be a consequence of a distant God. A distant God, similarly, might be the result of an unconnected God, one whose transcendence moves God right off our experiential maps. God always seems more "there" than "here"; given the likeliness of our disappointing God, perhaps that's where we needed God to be.

I wonder if the myriads of people who say they are "spiritual but not religious" are not, in fact, recoiling from the claustrophobic image of Christian life we have constructed. They don't want to be stuck in the past, trying to rectify things that keep recurring. They don't want a God staring from a far-off place or a God whose pickiness is hard to predict. They want a different challenge: to be part of a movement that partakes in God's work of bringing about the Kingdom. A vision that looks forward more than backward, calling for an optimism of common striving, will suit their vision of the world much better. Perhaps people today want the vastness that the image of the Kingdom can bring to their lives.

Living toward Tomorrow

To live as Christians means to live moving forward, to live toward the Kingdom. St. Paul sees Jesus pulling creation together into a Kingdom that he then hands over to the Father when God becomes "all in all." Because of the breakthrough of Jesus, the power of his resurrection already exists within creation. Paul describes Jesus as the "firstfruits"—the harvest has already begun with Jesus being the first of many who will live in the fulfillment of God, in that state where God is "all in all."

Yet such a vision might be hard to muster. A brief glance at the twentieth century, with its global wars, nuclear bombings, totalitarian governments, and battered climate, shows the availability of plenty of darkness. Starting the twenty-first century off with fanatical religious terrorism does not bode well for the century we are in right now, especially given a worldwide pandemic. This darkness in human life can easily seep into spirituality. Given recent experiences, we can easily imagine what the enormous death toll during the Black Plague did to Christian attitudes toward death. How absent must God have seemed when a third of humans died? But this darkness is not where Christians are called to dwell. Christians live not in the experience of absence but much more in one of presence.

Of course, Christians must live in and through many periods of darkness, but not as people who give in to it or, horribly, somehow profit from it. To live toward the Kingdom means assuming a prophetic voice, a witness's voice, against darkness and absence. When Christians sang "Maranatha" in the earliest centuries, the cry "Come, Lord Jesus" did not mean Jesus was absent; it meant that they sought the completion of a life they had already begun to live. Those who sing the loudest in the vision of heaven that the Book of Revelation gives us are those who "washed their robes and made them white in the blood of the Lamb" (Rev 7:14). To wash one's robes white with the blood of the Lamb can only mean to live with the same self-giving love that Jesus had when he came to live for, and bring about, the Kingdom. Indeed, as we shall see in chapter 7, that self-giving love is exactly what opens the future for humankind.

Living toward the future makes its own demands. As we recognize when we lean forward for any length of time, this can feel quite uncomfortable. Far easier is it to sit in loungers with our feet up and our muscles relaxed. To live

11

toward something implies a perpetual strain. Where we are is not where we are meant to be; rather, we lunge forward, eager to grasp a prize that somehow still eludes us. Again, from St. Paul: "I continue my pursuit toward the goal, the prize of God's upward calling, in Christ Jesus" (Phil 3:14).

"God's upward calling"—I suppose we have a choice here between feeling frustration or living in excitement. We can see God's "upward calling" as something that comes at the end of a miserable and often thankless trek, or we can view God's "upward calling" as the dynamic energy that constitutes our whole Christian life. We can live with assumptions and attitudes that seem to drag us back, or we can live with a vision that seems to pull us forward. We can choose the spirituality that speaks to our dreams.

I know when I am seeking or expecting something, I see it everywhere. When I go to the airport to greet a friend, I see my friend's face in almost everyone passing by. "Here she comes." "That's him walking toward me." Likewise, when I miss people deeply, I see them in so many places that I often have to shake my head to realize where they actually are. My love for those I seek and expect shapes the very vision of my eyes.

How true was the Flamingos' song "I Only Have Eyes for You" (1959). In a similar way, the longing, the forward thrust, the strain into the future is nothing less than the presence of the future shaping the moments in which we live; we come to only have eyes for what God is bringing about within us and between us. Those who have met Christ and begun to live in him through the Spirit only have eyes, really, for God and the Kingdom God wills as the goal of creation.

For all the energy we put into looking into the past, I think that the past does not necessarily have to loom larger in our minds than the future. Does yesterday have to have more power than tomorrow? Certainly, there's something limiting about yesterday. Not only has it slipped by, not only has it been congealed in memory; it also puts a fingerprint on our experience of today. Our genes or our past can seem like a limiting destiny. That's why we need the virtue of hope to train us to find power in tomorrow.

If we have no hope, then tomorrow is a frustrating joke as Macbeth puts it when he hears about the death of his wife in Shakespeare's famous play. Tomorrow can only creep, and its pace is petty. But if we live in hope, then we hear more clearly the boisterous singing of Annie, in the famous Broadway play, where tomorrow is "only a day away"—and the hope that the future can hold lifts the spirits of the whole audience.

It can be tempting to think of ourselves as caught between yesterday and tomorrow, passive like puppets on the strings of time. But time is hardly a passive construct, something we endure, ticks on a clock. Time is our actual life, in the historicity that defines who we are, inviting us to get on board, to give it direction. While we cannot, as St. Augustine shows in the final books of his *Confessions*, grasp and hold onto the moments that we have, so elusive are they, we can shape our time in accord with our intentions. These intentions can shut a vision down; or they can be the very DNA of the visions we are graced to have.

Tomorrow can, indeed, shape our lives even more than yesterday. For if yesterday can be limiting—how can I change the past?—tomorrow stands ripe with potential, with the possibilities that fuller experiences may yet be ours. While only a fool thinks life has no limitations, a yet bigger fool thinks that life has no potential for change, growth, or forward movement. That's what tomorrow means. Our stories are not ended; we've not exhausted things. Tomorrow says that every moment, which can seem like an ending, can be, even more, the beginning of something more.

~ • ~

Plopped as we are in time, every one of us lives to resolve the tension built into our lives. Faith is a way to deal with that tension, particularly the faith engendered by Jesus Christ who walks onto the stage of a Jewish desert to proclaim the coming of a Kingdom.

A spirituality toward tomorrow, a spirituality rich with potential for yet fuller futures, receives its energy from Jesus's announcement. Just as he took the layers of his Jewish life and faith, shaping them into a vision that ultimately shocked his contemporaries, so his words come to us with their own shock. "The Kingdom of God is at hand."

At hand. Coming. Right here. Toward. Tomorrow. The future.

The darkness of our December nights leads us to light Advent candles that mark the coming of something much more than a holiday or a feast. They can symbolize the point when time becomes the framework on which the Kingdom grows, when the layers of our experience come together, when the future emerges from within time.

Meditation: Layers of Existence

Sit in a room by yourself some afternoon, perhaps a sunlit room in winter. Just take the room in visually, noting the chairs, the walls, the windows, the sounds. Sit still and force yourself into a quiet that lets you observe, perceive, receive.

Although you see the things in the room—a table, a rug, a lamp—these things soon become more than themselves. The table is more than what you use to put things on; the rug is more than a covering for the floor. No, each of them takes on its own life, with its own story. The fabric, the construction, the installation, those who built and installed....

You hear the hiss of the radiator, or sense when a fan starts blowing the warm air. Is it gas? Is it oil? How many centuries was this fuel in preparation? What kind of history does it contain, of long-gone plains, vegetation now decomposing and combining, the earth's centuries-long pressure now compacted into fuel for your comfort? Note the light filtered by the glass. How far did it travel? Where did it originate and how long ago? What was involved in its formation, its composition, its refraction at its arrival at your windowpane?

You note the walls. Of what are they composed? What did the architect see when he drew on paper the shape of these walls? What feelings did he think the space would evoke, feelings of closeness, of light, of connection? Who were the workers who put up these walls? What were their histories? Immigrants each with a story of daring or desperation to tell? Who did they think of as they put up the wallboard and smoothed it out? Consider the eight or ten hours of manual labor, all so they could return home, their exhaustion absorbed by the smile of their spouses and the play of their children? Think of what's under the rug, the boards or tiles laid precisely by people who spent *half their lives on their knees, hoping their backs would hold out until retirement.*

Or the space you are in? Where is it in relation to the house, or the apartment, or the building, or the city in which you dwell? How we rotate through it without even noticing as earth spins in obedience to laws that perhaps we studied and knew more about at one point in our lives. Who else has been in this space? What were their stories or even histories like? The people who inhabited the place before it was yours...the families, the conversations, the arguments, the smiles, and tears. What forces shaped their lives? What forces shape your life?

Can you begin to count them? The physical laws that frame the space-time that we inhabit? The economic laws that made it likely that I live in this place at this point in my life? The relationships in terms of which I define myself? The stories I have come to tell myself about myself? The stories my parents told about themselves that embedded themselves somewhere, though unlocatable, inside me? The teachers who spontaneously jump into my mind when I think about this or read about that? The books that have shaped me? Not to mention the songs, plays, and movies?

What are the forces in my own experience—my earliest friends, the first sensations I had that sometimes return with a taste of soup or ice cream, the shames I was forced to feel, the fame I tried to claim, the games I lost and those I managed to win? Who was the first person I loved, though I barely knew the word back then? The infatuations I had? The fears I had of rejection? The desires of attraction that drove me? What did that first hug mean, the first kiss, the first sense of some extraordinary feeling that, once born, only seemed to grow?

Did you notice how beautiful something seemed? Was it the plant in the corner, or the angle of the chairs, or a painting on the wall? Why do you feel so at home in this space? If, somehow, you returned a thousand years from now, don't you feel you'd remember this moment exactly: the inner feeling, the smells, the wonder. The wonder, indeed: How did this room get here? These things? Why do they exist? Nothing has to be and, yet, here it is...here you are! Go anywhere your imagination ranges, beyond planets or beneath oceans. Would your curiosity die? Or would your mind not want to penetrate, perk with more questions, pound with theories and ideas? No matter where we go, surprise! There is meaning to be had, thoughts to conjure, desires that arise.

A meaning everywhere, before and beyond the things that are, a meaning sweeping and embracing....And, believe it, an ultimately loving meaning, for there is no other way the graciousness of our existence could begin and perdure without that. You sense it, perhaps as a layer around all the other layers, not a separate layer but one that penetrates everything, whether waves, or particles, or atoms, or electrons; whether patterns, or pieces, or clusters, or organisms, or life dynamics, or sense, or mind. You sense it, a love whispered before time, by a self-diffusive Lover.

Connected, related, layered, limited but dynamic, emerging in surprise, emerging in Love.

Every single second of our lives seems to touch all of time and space.

Every single second of our lives can open us to the multiple layers that compose our one human experience.

~ • ~

17

For Reflection and Discussion

Read this passage slowly.

Matthew 21:23–27

When [Jesus] had come into the temple area, the chief priests and the elders of the people approached him as he was teaching and said, "By what authority are you doing these things? And who gave you this authority?" Jesus said to them in reply, "I shall ask you one question, and if you answer it for me, then I shall tell you by what authority I do these things. Where was John's baptism from? Was it of heavenly or of human origin?" They discussed this among themselves and said, "If we say 'Of heavenly origin,' he will say to us, 'Then why did you not believe him?' But if we say, 'Of human origin,' we fear the crowd, for they all regard John as a prophet." So they said to Jesus in reply, "We do not know." He himself said to them, "Neither shall I tell you by what authority I do these things."

1. What are the questions people raise today that allow them not to have to encounter or deal with Jesus?
2. What do I imagine is the spirituality of the religious leaders who are questioning Jesus? What were their assumptions?
3. In what ways have I declined to see the hand of God in something because of its implications in my life? How many times have I not acted because of fear?

Slowly pray the Lord's Prayer and conclude by asking God's blessing on you and yours.

Chapter 2

━━━━━━━━━━

PROCLAIMING
THE KINGDOM

IF I COULD GO BACK in time and witness a scene from the life of Jesus, which one would it be?

Just from the images and statues that Christians have developed over the years, the crucifixion might seem to come in first. Even Protestants who do not like the way Catholics put the corpus of Jesus on the crucifix still retain the cross as their basic symbol. People flocked to see Mel Gibson's movie The Passion of the Christ: *our modern version of medieval pilgrimages to the Holy Land when the devout traveled far in order to walk the path of Jesus's final journey toward death. In this, Christians were only reprising an ancient curiosity about Jesus's death, one going back to traditions about St. Helena, mother of Emperor Constantine, who could find no rest until she found the true cross.*

Others might opt for the Last Supper even though it was probably nothing like Leonardo da Vinci's famous painting. Certainly some might opt for the raising of Lazarus, told with such sustained drama by John (John 11:1ff.), until Jesus, at the climax, finally cries out, "Lazarus, come out." The very curious among us might choose one of the several scenes where the bread is multiplied;

Jesus recites the blessing, gives the food to his disciples to pass out, and, wow!, five thousand people have bread and fish. Another near-top finisher would be the transfiguration, those seemingly timeless seconds when the physical brilliance of Jesus stuns his followers.

But my pick would be the start of Jesus's public ministry, after his baptism and after his time of being tested in the desert. I would choose the way Luke tells it in his Gospel because of how it is tied into a long Jewish prophetic tradition going back to Isaiah. I'd want to see the faces of Jesus's hometowners as he makes his way to the local meeting house for prayer, and the expectation they had when they handed him the scroll of Isaiah to read. Was this just some ordinary event, something that happened quite often? Was Jesus already such a town favorite that he would often be asked to read? Was this like an altar server coming back to the parish after going away to college? "Would you mind serving today?"

I'd love to see the faces when Jesus picked out what must have been an often-used passage near the end of Isaiah and then sat down. Why do their eyes fix on him? What else are they feeling? And, just like that, Jesus says it: "Today this scripture passage is fulfilled in your hearing" (Luke 4:21).

~ • ~

Luke's Gospel substantially amplifies what we see in Matthew and Mark concerning the proclamation of Jesus's initial message.

As Luke presents it, Jesus moves from being tempted in the desert to starting his mission in Galilee, his home province. Something different is already happening in Jesus's life because Luke refers to the power of the Spirit being with Jesus and how "news of him spread throughout the whole region" (Luke 4:14). Teaching in various synagogues, he finally comes to his hometown synagogue in Nazareth, where he seems to be already well known. Asked to read, the townspeople give Jesus the scroll of the prophet Isaiah.

"He unrolled the scroll and found the passage where it was written: 'The Spirit of the Lord is upon me.'" Jesus did not have to unroll the scroll very much because this passage is near the end of Isaiah, the section of the book that was originally addressed to the Jewish people who were in exile in Babylon. Perhaps the implication concerns the ongoing exile that besets all human life, an exile that Jesus was about to address.

The passage from Isaiah has become so familiar to us that we might overlook the stark boldness and power that Isaiah's words evoke:

> The Spirit of the Lord is upon me,
>   because he has anointed me
>   to bring glad tidings to the poor.
> He has sent me to proclaim liberty to captives
>   and recovery of sight to the blind,
>   to let the oppressed go free,
> and to proclaim a year acceptable to the Lord.
>   (Luke 4:18–19)

How should we hear these words of Isaiah that Jesus makes his own? How would they have been heard by people who were experiencing military occupation by the Roman Empire? How would the people of Nazareth have understood Jesus's reference to the "poor"? Did they see themselves as poor? Did they suppose Jesus was talking about them or was he speaking of others who would be helped?

The words are revolutionary. Jesus is "anointed"—which means a formal designation by God—to bring good news to the poor, to people who do not think they have anything and, perhaps, do not even think they deserve anything. In fact, the passage adds a bit of precision to the idea of "poor" by telling us the kinds of people who will be addressed: captives who need liberty, blind people who need sight, and oppressed people who will find freedom.

All of this is happening at a special point in time for which Jesus uses Isaiah's words: "a year acceptable to the Lord." In other words, this is like a jubilee year of grace and forgiveness, a period of starting anew and liberation, which Jesus inaugurates in his hometown. Jesus's ministry would be marked by events unique in his time but also in all of history. Jesus was doing something new on behalf of God, something coterminous with his own life.

Initially the hometown crowd liked what Jesus had to say. The passage continues in this way: "Rolling up the scroll, he handed it back to the attendant and sat down, and the eyes of all in the synagogue looked intently at him. He said to them, 'Today this scripture passage is fulfilled in your hearing.' And all spoke highly of him and were amazed at the gracious words that came from his mouth" (Luke 4:20–22). Jesus is making time something special: history is now coming to a junction; Jesus will pull history forward toward a destiny latent within it. Time takes on a direction that points to mercy and grace.

We can sense this in the utterly audacious sentence that comes next, when Jesus tells his hometown neighbors that Isaiah's astounding prophecy is being fulfilled at the very moment his words reach their ears. "Today," Jesus begins, with a word that refers to the most immediate point of time available to us. This very moment, this very instant that you have right now in your life, this "today" of your life, now carries a fulfillment way beyond itself. It's a fulfillment now available in their immediate experience. It's as undeniable as the syllables of Jesus's words hitting their ears.

Kingdom

We will have to return to this scene at a later point. We should not miss, however, the opportunity to compare this scene with the one Mark presents.

> After John had been arrested, Jesus came to Gali-
> lee proclaiming the gospel of God. "This is the time
> of fulfillment. The kingdom of God is at hand.
> Repent, and believe in the gospel." (Mark 1:14)

Once again, Jesus's message is presented as "gospel" or as "good news" and "glad tidings." A time of fulfillment has come; history has come to its destiny. Something is going to happen because the Kingdom of God is "at hand." The energy that longtime expectation generates bursts forth at this point. We are on the verge of something totally transformative. Jesus describes this by a term he will use throughout the Gospels: "Kingdom of God."

Given the language of Luke and what we will see throughout all the Gospels, certain possible meanings to the word *kingdom* need to be excluded. Israel had a long and rather tortured experience of kingship for more than four hundred years. Despite the way the Scriptures extol King David, for the most part Jewish kings were losers. Immediately after David comes his son, Solomon, who, given the privilege of building the first Jewish Temple, proceeds on a course of idolatry. Marrying into the families of the tribes that surround the Jewish people, Solomon adopts the gods and religious styles of these tribes. So great are Solomon's sins that, immediately after his reign, the nation that David had unified now split into two different parts, each with its own king, never to be united again.

However much Jewish thinking might idealize the thought of kingship, the fact is that after the exile in Babylon (580 BC) when the Jewish people returned to Jerusalem, there never was another king. Instead, Jewish people had to endure one foreign occupation after another until, at the time of Jesus, it was the Romans who had taken them over. While it might be possible for some of Jesus's hearers to think that he was claiming some new political power in the face of Roman occupation, nothing in Jesus's ministry shows anything like that. Indeed, any time people were tempted to invest Jesus with political power, he found a way to disappear (see, e.g., John 6:15).

If Jesus does not have the ancient Jewish kingship in mind when he proclaims the coming of the Kingdom, neither does he have what many Christians have constructed over the centuries—the idea of the Kingdom as a nonearthly, ethereal world populated by souls who, by some philosophical trick, are somehow able to wear white robes and play harps. This "spirit" world would make little sense to Jews of the first century. As we saw, although some Jews did not believe in resurrection, most did believe in it. But all of them understood by the term "resurrection" that humans would have a bodily life; none of them thought that heaven meant not having human, corporal existence.

So what did Jesus mean when he spoke of the Kingdom of God? Quite obviously what he says in Luke's Gospel,

24

because this is exactly what he goes about doing in his ministry. Jesus sees himself as one who brings about in the lives of people that liberation and wholeness that reflects God's will. In Mark's Gospel, right after he announces the Kingdom, Jesus embarks on calling apostles, healing people possessed by demons, curing people who are ill, and inviting those people that respectable Jewish society would not have invited—tax collectors and prostitutes. Jesus shows us, in his actions, what the term "Kingdom of God" means for him.

The Kingdom Jesus referred to was a way of life marked by a new understanding of God as Father and a new way of relating to other people because of the Father's love. What were characteristics of Jesus's Kingdom? A list might look like this:

Accepting God as our loving Father
Proclaiming good news to the poor
Healing the afflicted
Working for justice for humankind
Freeing the imprisoned
Including the excluded
Demonstrating forgiveness of sin
Giving life to the dead
Living a life based on prayer

It's as if Jesus looked at the hopes that have been embedded in human experience from the beginning and pronounced those hopes to be valid and worthy of fulfillment.

This list has to sober everyone who reads it because it still stands, even today, as a challenge yet to be fulfilled. Some two millennia after Jesus, his project, his life's ministry, still remains unattained. Certainly, people today could point to some progress in various areas, perhaps in the area of better health or a wider spread of democratic systems. But Jesus's optimism at this first moment of his ministry can certainly appear as still unaccomplished.

Opposition

We know that the emergence of the Kingdom contained some very disagreeable elements. In other words, the Kingdom does not come by everyone accepting Jesus's words and a new world suddenly springing into existence. Rather, from the beginning, Jesus's vision is fraught with contention. As it turns out, this contentious opposition would be a major factor on how the Kingdom finally is revealed.

Notice how Mark's passage begins: "After John had been arrested" (1:14). John the Baptist had begun preaching some time before Jesus, offering baptism as a sign of people wanting to change their lives and be prepared for what God would soon bring about. In fact, Matthew's Gospel has John proclaiming something quite close to Jesus: "Repent, for the kingdom of heaven is at hand!" (Matt 3:2). John evoked the oldest prophetic traditions of the Jewish people, ones like Elijah and Elisha who, preaching at a time of disbelief and corruption, called people to a radical reorientation of themselves to God.

John the Baptist, however, has already been arrested; we know that he will subsequently be murdered by Herod (Mark 6:17–29). Jesus seems to want to take up John's message and infuse his own distinct voice of hope into it. It is as if Jesus fully acknowledges the tradition of martyrdom and seems willing to apply it to himself. How

would his rejection and death be part of the proclaiming
of glad tidings, of pronouncing healing and liberation for
people?

This same sentiment of rejection is also present in
the scene we began with, Jesus's appearance in his hometown synagogue, flush with the vigorous words of Isaiah.
Immediately after his townsmen express admiration for
his gracious words, the very words that were being fulfilled as they heard them, we hear a very different note:

> They also asked, "Isn't this the son of Joseph?"
> He said to them, "Surely you will quote me this
> proverb, 'Physician, cure yourself....'" And he
> said, "Amen, I say to you, no prophet is accepted
> in his own native place...." They rose up, drove
> him out of the town, and led him to the brow of
> the hill on which their town had been built, to
> hurl him down headlong. But he passed through
> the midst of them and went away. (Luke 4:22bff.)

It becomes clear that the coming of the Kingdom of God,
announced with such optimism at the beginning, would
not happen until Jesus faced the most dreaded parts of
human experience: opposition, rejection, violence, and
even execution. In effect, Jesus becomes the poor, the
captive, the imprisoned, and the crippled so that these
might be vindicated when he is raised from the dead.

The Kingdom, then, is a vision of transformed humankind, initiated as a time of grace and favor by God, in which
the brokenness and sin of human existence would be overcome by the mercy God shows us in and through Jesus's
death and resurrection.

Neither an ancient political kingdom nor some celes-
tial spa, the Kingdom Jesus announces is the victory God

brings about in human history to advance its fulfillment. Accepting Jesus's message means committing oneself to the same vision he had, to engender deeds of hope and life especially for the poor and ignored—and to do so as a sign of history's advance toward its fulfillment. Accepting Jesus's message means consciously participating in the transformation of human existence.

Conversion

The traditions from Mark and Matthew initiate Jesus's message with a word translated by "repent." This translation seems to shortchange the scope of meaning for the Greek word *metanoiete*. It is certainly true that the word can mean "repent" in the sense of turning one's back on something or changing one's mind. But the word seems pregnant with a fuller meaning, one that probably brings out Jesus's meaning with a lot more emphasis.

Part of the Greek word (*noia*) that translates Jesus's message means our "minds" or our mentality. This is a way to talk about the images and visions that we develop in our lives, things that come to shape our actions. How many of us, for example, have developed stories about ourselves that trap us or keep us from stretching ourselves or even, for some, keeping ourselves from feeling loved? How many of us are trapped by stories that others tell of us—that we were not good enough, or that we could never really compete, or that we were going nowhere? We can think back to our childhood classes in school and the implicit roles that some students took on—who was going to be the bright one, or the student with the most friends, or the class clown, or the smart aleck, or the one who seemed to have more money than any of the other students.

These visions we develop—whether as individuals or as societies—help us see some things, but they can certainly block our seeing many other things. A society that assumes the superiority of one race or language group is never able to easily see those who are "other." A society that bases itself on the acquisition of money interprets its success, and views its members, in a certain way. A person unable to be cured of narcissism continues to think that everyone else revolves around her or his life. Such are the mental pictures that can hold us in their sway.

The other part of the Greek word the Gospel uses (*meta*) means something like "over"—in the sense that our minds can be turned over or around. The idea is that our visions can be turned upside down so that we can come to see life in a very different way. "Turn your hearts over" or "turn your brain upside down" come closer to what Jesus was inviting people to do in his day.

Of course, there is also a turning away involved in this idea. People are invited to turn away from at least parts of the vision that they have been using to understand themselves and their world. Some of the things to turn away from might involve outright sin—the way we use others for pleasure or gain or power. Others might be tendencies that can lead to sin, and perhaps even compromises people have made with themselves or their communities. How easy to end up with a distorted way of relating; how almost impossible it can be to change!

But maybe the invitation to repent—to turn away from something toward something else—is Jesus's way of inviting us to turn our back on all the static and clunky ways we have viewed ourselves. Indeed, is not Jesus saying that we need to turn over our mentalities precisely to even see the Kingdom? So the conversion Jesus asks of his followers is to turn their vision from most of the things that occupy us in a limited timeframe and toward the one reality that should claim our whole attention: toward the Kingdom, toward that future in which God's reign is shown by the way we help bring each other, through God's mercy, to the fullness that our lives cry out for.

In Mark's phrasing of Jesus's initial message, there is another word that is part of the conversion Jesus invites his followers to have. "Repent, and believe in the gospel" (Mark 1:15). Different religious traditions have different approaches to "belief" or "faith." The Catholic tradition seems to have emphasized the content of belief, namely, the Creed and the elements of faith, which we accept because of our trust in the God who endorses them, as the First Vatican Council (1870) put it. Martin Luther and many following in his Protestant tradition emphasize the idea of trust, that our Christian lives are ultimately a total reliance on God. So personal decision enjoys a prominent place, along with the various doctrines of faith.

But "faith" at the time of Jesus could also mean fidelity. We have faith when we are faithful to someone or something in which we believe. This idea adds a further tone to the initial proclamation of the Kingdom that Jesus makes. We are to turn our faces toward a future that he proclaims and inaugurates, and, coming to live for the future, we are to remain faithful to the vision that Jesus announces. Fidelity demands action, the constant looking out for what is needed, for what can help. The temptation to contract the Kingdom into something more provincial or more convenient undermines the spirituality that Jesus offers his followers.

In other words, if being spiritual means coming to live for a vision that grounds the assumptions and goals of our lives, then being a person of faith means keeping that vision as an energizing and organizing force in our own lives.

The disciple follows Jesus, allowing the vision of Jesus to direct our actions toward a fullness that God has promised us, and has inaugurated for us, in Jesus.

~ • ~

I've been puzzled at how quickly the hometown, in Luke's narration, turns against Jesus. The point of their disappointment seems to be Jesus's very ordinariness: isn't he just a local boy, don't we know his family, or, maybe more pointed, who does he think he is? But this criticism of Jesus seals the deal, as I think about it. The potential to shape life toward a future, freeing it from a relentless past that drags things down, can spring up anywhere, even ancient Galilee. The human mind has, at any point, the potential to change its perspective. The human heart has no inherent barriers to its desire to love. God's grace can touch us at every point.

How many times have I let past limitations define what I think can happen in my life? How many ways have I seen people stumped by the images they have of themselves, unable to turn their minds around and see something new? "Come on," I say, "it doesn't have to be that way." But how often have I seen it take years for something to break through; even, unfortunately, almost a lifetime?

The ordinariness of Jesus, which caused repudiation by his neighbors, underlines the extraordinariness of our ordinary lives. If Jesus can break through time and inertia, he can bring us along with him. The Kingdom is starting in a new, vibrant way.

Let's see how Jesus goes about it.

Meditation: One of the Townsfolk

I was happy to see Jesus return to town the other day. He seemed as familiar as ever, though he had a few new people who were following him, being his companions. I was in the synagogue when he was invited to read the Scripture. And I was very familiar with the selection he picked.

What surprised me was the intensity with which he spoke, as if something had dawned on him and he could not shake it. The tone of his voice and the way he stood before us, as if he wanted to lead us to a new place we had not been before....I gasped, like everyone, when he said that Isaiah's famous prophecy was being fulfilled in our very lives, in our very hearing of Jesus's words.

What, after all, was going to be different? How could Nazareth and the surrounding towns be expected to change? Weren't we the same people we had always been? Had not we come to settle for the existence that God gave us, one of ordinary work, some close friends, and neighbors we had come to know all too well. It was dramatic, sure, and gripping. But what, in the end, could it mean?

I wasn't happy when the sniping came from my neighbors. It's as if we think our job is to keep everyone in his or her place, to keep the town, to keep our lives, exactly as we had found them. "Isn't he the carpenter's son?" Indeed, so that would disqualify him from reading Isaiah and believing in those words we so often, ourselves, have brushed aside? "We know his kin," they said, as if he could be defined only by who his people were.

I had a sense, when they shoved him out to the cliff on which our town was built, that they were really running away from the possibility that their lives could mean more than they presently do. I had a sense they were terrified to think they were important to God, to history, or to anything else. Let's throw away our prophets that bring us hope—because it's more comfortable to live without hope. It's more comfortable to accept things as they are and have been.

I know they wanted to get rid of Jesus. I just don't know why they always choose to live without hope.

~ • ~

For Reflection and Discussion

Read this passage slowly and reflectively.

1 John 1:1–4

What was from the beginning,
   what we have heard,
   what we have seen with our eyes,
   what we looked upon
   and touched with our hands
   concerns the Word of life—
for the life was made visible;
   we have seen it and testify to it
   and proclaim to you the eternal life
   that was with the Father and was made visible to us—
what we have seen and heard
   we proclaim now to you,
   so that you too may have fellowship with us;
   for our fellowship is with the Father
   and with his Son, Jesus Christ.
We are writing this so that our joy may be complete.

1. If you tried to summarize how you imagine Jesus, what words would you use?

2. How often do you think of your faith life as a meeting, an encounter, with Jesus? How could this be happening more?

3. In what ways would you describe the life that you have in common with Jesus, that is, what you feel Jesus has given to you in your faith life?

Slowly pray the Lord's Prayer and conclude by asking God's blessing on you and yours.

Chapter 3

ENACTING THE KINGDOM

I THINK ONE OF the most difficult dimensions of life is actually doing something.

I may have dreamed and desired something for years, but perhaps I never actually got off the sofa to make it happen. I have looked back at the gaps in my life, my abysmal abilities in math, for example: "Maybe I should go online and learn calculus?" I think. But doing more tasks in the office, or playing Solitaire on my Kindle, or duffing more golf balls always seems more important.

This is different from procrastination because, as I've come to observe, procrastinators know their procrastination; they can call it that because, in the end, they actually turn in the article or finish the task. Getting started just seems to be their problem. While procrastinators eventually get things done, I'm talking about the phenomenon of never getting around to something, never bringing something about. The fantasy was as good as the reality.

Spiritual writers have fancy words for this like *acedia* or *abulia*. Perhaps more contemporary elements of depression need to enter the conversation as well. We have so many ways of thinking of how things just don't get done, various kinds of gridlock in our private and public lives. Maybe some kind of depression lies behind our modern need to elect people who only oppose each other and, thus, never get anything done that can claim the allegiance of most citizens.

But Jesus, once he proclaimed the Kingdom, had no such problem. He went about doing the deeds to show what he meant without wasting a moment.

~ • ~

Historians frequently comment on the New Testament of Thomas Jefferson, one of America's prominent founding fathers. Jefferson was part of a movement that felt that some of the Christian story seemed legendary or even magical. Since that generation of leaders were heavily influenced by the Enlightenment and the subsequent Industrial Revolution, it felt little need to keep prominent stories or ideas that corresponded little with their contemporary experience of scientific achievement and political reorganization.

Jefferson, accordingly, cut from his New Testament those passages that showed anything like the deeds of Jesus, particularly his miracles. The words of Jesus, their wisdom and perspective, seemed most important to Jefferson and his peers. As a result, Jefferson's Bible was a collection of Jesus's words and parables. Jesus's project might merit reflection and discussion, but it didn't deserve any particular kind of commitment. In this way, the Kingdom came as an idea but not as something that needed to be enacted, that demanded action.

Paradoxically, since the time of Jefferson, modern scholars have discovered an ancient manuscript tradition called the Gospel of Thomas. This tradition, which dates to sometime in the first century, was discovered in 1945 when archeologists found a trove of ancient documents in a cave in Egypt near Nag Hammadi. Thomas's so-called Gospel has never been part of the accepted Christian canon of Scriptures. Nevertheless, what's interesting about this Gospel is that it is basically just words, just sayings. Someone collected a group of sayings attributed to Jesus (about half of the sayings in the Gospel of Thomas are also, in fact, in the New Testament), anticipating, in a strange way, the skeptics that would emerge centuries later around the time of the Enlightenment.

Something about Jefferson's approach appeals to modern people. We have become skeptical kinds of folks, applauding the doubts of Thomas the Apostle after Jesus's resurrection and feeling more comfortable with our faith being something more like wisdom or attitude. The risk in this approach, of course, is that one can have a wisdom or attitude that takes life as it comes, that basically endorses or frames our limited experience. Wisdom, attitude, perspective does not have to look to the future, to tomorrow, to dreams yet to come about. It can content itself with what's before its face, make some appropriate comments, and it can do so on its own terms.

But this is far from the attitude of Jesus.

Signs and Wonders

Despite the scissors of Thomas Jefferson, much of the Bible does revolve around remarkable actions, whether it's the escape of the Jewish people from Egypt in the Book of Exodus, or the resurrection of Jesus in the New Testament. Amazing deeds also accompanied some of the actions of certain prophets, particularly Elijah and Elisha. Some people think that Jesus modeled his own ministry on those ancient Jewish prophets. But all of this raises questions for us because we have been trained to ask "how" and to look for some visible chain of causality. If it rains that's because one front of air with moisture hit another front of air that was either colder or warmer. If the sun comes up, that's because the inertia of gravity keeps the earth spinning and moving around the sun with regularity every day. So how, mechanistically, did these wonders happen?

I wonder, though, if focusing on the "how" of causality might be a distraction from what the Scriptures want to tell us. I say this above and beyond the obvious fact that no one of us understands all the laws or nature or all the patterns of causality even in our daily lives. No one of us can comprehend the richness of even a moment of her or his life, as we saw in the meditation at the end of chapter 1. But even apart from the limitations of our knowledge, the Scriptures might not be speaking so much about how things work as to what things are trying to show. This means that the purpose of wonders and deeds is to focus our attention on deeper things that God does in our lives, on other levels of reality, things that we do not often pay attention to or, even worse, can actually resist.

For if the deeds of God are meant to point to the Kingdom, then are we not in danger of missing something crucial and important if we feel we can dismiss the deeds out of hand?

The word *miracle* might be instructive itself. Part of its root has the meaning "to see," to look at something, to look at something that causes us to question or to wonder. These ideas are so close that ancient Greek used the same word (*thaumazein*) for both wonder and puzzlement; in other words, if something makes us wonder or makes us scratch our heads, then it stands out from the everyday run of things. The basic sense of miracle has less to do with the how of causality and much more to do with exceptional wonders that point us to something beyond the expected, that ultimately point us to God.

This seems to have been part of the method of Jesus. He not only had a message; he performed actions that caused people to be puzzled and filled with wonder. Some people saw this as an elaboration of God's action in our world; others saw this as manipulation or even a demonic acting. One of Jesus's frequent deeds was driving demons from people. We might have a variety of modern ways to think about demonic possession today (e.g., psychological categories like depression or schizophrenia) but that's almost beside the point. Jesus showed God's power against forces that were associated with destruction and evil; in this way he revealed God's intentions, in the categories of his ancient culture, to free our world and bring it to fulfillment. He was attacked for this by religious leaders who said that it was through demonic power that Jesus drove out demons. He rebuts their attack and then adds, tellingly, "But if it is by the finger of God that [I] drive out demons, then the kingdom of God has come upon you" (Luke 11:20).

God's Kingdom erupts into human awareness by the very deeds that Jesus does. These deeds, however the causality worked, made people stop, look, and take notice. Their attention then led them to an openness to God's power in their lives and their world, an openness that pushed them toward a vision of hope for different possibilities in their lives.

In a way, one can think of the miraculous, as a category, as indicating the way even present time points to, and contains, a fullness yet to come. If we strive toward a Kingdom, a new tomorrow, when sin, illness, hatred, isolation, and brutality will exist no more, then that very striving might bring these future hopes into present experience. We can see the miraculous even in the wonders of daily life.

Another way to think of the miraculous points to the various layers of experience we reflected on in chapter 1. Every moment of experience is so intertwined with every other moment of existence. What we can see and analyze amounts to only a slice of the multilayered reality that we are and that we live in. This becomes totally clear when, for example, a parent hugs a child. The mother or father cannot come up with words adequate enough to explain what just happened and all that it meant. The miraculous are these deeper, latent layers showing themselves more clearly in our experience.

Gathering

Jesus never seems to have viewed his project, inaugurating the Kingdom of God, as something he did alone. Of course, Jesus saw everything he did with reference to his Father. He frames his life in terms of obeying his Father; he flatly states, "I came down from heaven not to do my own will but the will of the one who sent me" (John 6:38). We can see this obedience of Jesus as constant openness to what he understands his Father is calling him to do. Rather than being a passive following of the will of the Father, it is an active engagement with what Jesus sees his Father is all about.

Similarly, the Holy Spirit attended every moment and action of Jesus. In fact, the Gospels see the Holy Spirit as sparking the mission of Jesus. When Jesus accepts baptism at the hand of John, the Spirit appears in the form of a dove (Mark 1:10); was this a sign of the peace Jesus would strive to bring during his ministry? Maybe, too, it was a sign of the renewed creation God was bringing about, referring to the dove that Noah sent out after the flood (Gen 8:8). But, right after his baptism, it is the Spirit who leads Jesus into the desert to prepare for his mission (Mark 1:12).

Most notable about Jesus's mission is the way it begins: he calls people to gather around him, to be his disciples, and to share in his ministry. Matthew and Mark have Jesus walking along the Galilean seashore, seeing fishermen at work. These are the folks he initially calls to be part of his band of followers (Mark 1:16–20). Soon enough, however, we begin reading about the crowds who are gathering about Jesus, people anxious to hear his word. We also read about a group of women who followed Jesus (Luke 8:2–3). I do not suppose his calling these women was any less dramatic than his calling the original fishermen from Galilee; in fact, these women displayed a faithfulness to Jesus that far exceeded that of the apostles (Luke 24:10).

This aspect of enacting the Kingdom is bad news for one of the dominant attitudes that people have developed about faith, the thought that it is a personal thing between "me and God" or "me and Jesus." That might be convenient for those who think their spirituality is already formed, that they have no more to learn and no need to interact with people: "I've been saved." But the growth that the followers of Jesus experienced happened as they interacted with Jesus and with each other because we are never finished forming our spiritual lives. We are never done growing in our following of Jesus. The Kingdom always stands ahead of us, calling us forward in our lives.

This aspect reveals another essential dimension of the Kingdom: it is based on invitation. It is inherently missionary. Much of the growth of the Kingdom may seem automatic, like Jesus's image of the farmer who wakes up and sees his crops have grown but does not know how (Mark 4:26). But the Kingdom also calls for direct invitation, as when Jesus sends out the twelve apostles and then a further seventy-two disciples (Luke 9 and 10). Sending that number of disciples was a clear message because the Jewish people thought there were seventy-two Gentile nations. Christ's message goes out to Israel, but it also goes out to the world.

Cana

The purpose of miracles stands out in a special way in the Gospel of John in which the first *sign* (the word John uses for what we call "miracle") Jesus does revolves around helping a young couple have a successful wedding party. We might well feel that this is not the kind of emergency that demanded special divine power, but the surprise of Jesus's first miracle, helping a wedding couple recover their dignity, might well reveal the importance of this sign. Jesus is going to begin something; he might as well start it there, in Cana, for this couple. Perhaps this is why John puts this sign as the first of the ones he will talk about. Signs are not about emergencies; they are about showing the inner reality of God to people who need to see it.

There are two intersecting areas of drama in the story we find in the second chapter of the Gospel of John. One area involves the people connected to the wedding, including the couple, the headwaiter and the other waiters, and the various servants and guests. The other area involves Jesus, his mother Mary, and his disciples. The wedding party is concerned about their lack of preparation for the wedding feast; Jesus and Mary are concerned about the unfolding of his life.

Mary asks Jesus to notice that the party has run out of wine. She asks him for his first sign. Jesus seems to acknowledge the importance of Mary's request because, in effect, he puts her request off. "Woman, how does your concern affect me? My hour has not yet come" (John 2:4). Jesus is patently aware of the enormity of his first step. Things would unfold from the first sign that he accomplishes, things that would define his destiny, his "hour." The word *hour* hardly refers to time. We will find that word later in the Gospel of John when it refers to Jesus's passion: "Jesus knew that his hour had come to pass from this world to the Father" (John 13:1). What happened in that little town would open up events that led to his death on Mt. Calvary.

The drama of Jesus's conversation with his mother merges with the drama of the unprepared party. The sheer magnitude of Jesus's sign demands all our attention. Taking the water jars used for purification of feet, six of them that could hold twenty to thirty gallons each, to the head waiter, the servants realize what Jesus has done. All those gallons of water have become wine! We do not need to take out our calculators to figure how much wine Jesus made. Nor is the point the chemical process by which water might become wine. No, the point is the abundance of wine, a sign of the joy and revelry that God would pour upon all humankind through the ministry of Jesus.

In fancier words, this is an apocalyptic sign, a sign of the end-times when creation will receive the fullness of God's gifts, becoming a dancing feast of joy. This sign points to the kind of future God envisions for humankind. The Gospel says that Jesus "revealed his glory" by this first sign; this began the process whereby the disciples came to believe in him (John 2:11). It also began the process by which creation would move more clearly toward its goal. Jesus's hour is the hour of creation itself.

However much Christians have emphasized sadness and suffering in their piety, in one form or another, through so many expressions of Christian faith, this first sign calls Jesus's disciples to an exultant joy because the abundance of God's life is beginning to come upon humankind. Take off that face of doom and gloom; put aside the fire and brimstone. Let go of the scruples you think God uses to torture you. Life is meant to be a feast where the wine never runs out!

This sign not only looks forward to Jesus's resurrection; it looks, even more, to the bestowal of the Holy Spirit on humankind, a Spirit that guides us into an ever-richer future. John intends us to look at everything else in his Gospel as an instance of this abundance, as if the wine of joy would overflow through the rest of the acts of Jesus. John, assumed to be the latest of the Gospels to be written, would naturally also see that overflow in the Christian life that had already resulted from the sending of the Holy Spirit.

Enacting the Kingdom begins by being filled with an irrepressible Spirit of joy.

~ • ~

The spilling of the joy of Cana through the actions of Jesus took on many forms. Near the end of the Gospel of John we see these words: "Now Jesus did many other signs in the presence of [his] disciples that are not written in this book. But these are written that you may [come to] believe that Jesus is the Messiah, the Son of God, and that through this belief you may have life in his name" (John 20:30–31).

Most of the signs that Jesus did, even those gestures that form the basis of our sacraments, had a distinct purpose. They freed people who were otherwise caught or stuck. They freed people from a past or a present that had blocked them from a future. Jesus liberated them precisely so they could begin to engage this future. Among the effects of Jesus's signs, we see healing, forgiveness, restoring, and inclusion of others. These indicate the kind of activities that should characterize the actions of Jesus's followers.

These actions of Jesus, bringing so much joy to people freed from what limited and trapped them, harken to the kind of joyful, sign-filled life that should mark all of Christian life. Repent, yes; sacrifice and fast; confess and reform—but all of these serve mostly to dispose us to joy!

Healing

Early in his Gospel, Mark gives us a striking story that deals not only with healing, but also with the purpose of healing.

There were, of course, many thousands of people in need of healing in Jewish territory at the time of Jesus, not to mention people throughout the world. This fact forces us to look upon all the stories of healing as emblematic: they intend to show God's intention toward all of humankind. None of the healings stands on its own; each stands as an instance of a ministry of Jesus that would set the stage for the behavior of his followers. Disciples for the

Kingdom commit themselves to healing others even more than to being healed. For do we not have the capacity to heal because of our own need for healing?

The story we find in chapter 3 of Mark's Gospel goes out of its way to show that the man, who suffered from a withered hand, was intended to be made an example. As the scene opens, Jesus has entered a synagogue "again"; this word lets us know that Jesus had formed a pattern that others had picked up on. And so, the stage was set for Jesus to show us what healing meant.

Even this early in his ministry, Jesus had engendered opposition from certain religious leaders, notably the Pharisees. Christians often misread Pharisees as religious phonies, but their main impulse was not showing off their faith so much as living their faith as fully as they could in daily life. These people were, then, the most pious of folks in Israel at the time of Jesus.

Can we be trapped by even our own piety? Surely, we can make almost anything into a trap, but the issue in the healing that Mark presents to us outlines a particularly vicious kind of trap. What happens when our own piety, that is, our own sense of religious connection to God, prevents us from encountering God in reality? What happens when our own approach to God obscures the very dimension of God we need to see? Surely this comes as a warning for all our distorted forms of piety.

As Mark presents the healing, we get the feeling that there have been previous discussions between Jesus and the local Pharisees. Perhaps that's the sense of "again" that starts the story: "Again he entered the synagogue" (Mark 3:1). The man with the withered hand seems also to have frequented the synagogue in the past. Who knows if he prayed out loud about his handicap? Who knows if people in the synagogue had interpreted his disability for him, perhaps insinuating that there must be some sin to have caused this in his life? Who knows if he mostly came to beg?

At any rate, the religious leaders are watching both Jesus and the crippled man. "They watched him closely to see if he would cure him on the sabbath so they might accuse him" (3:2). Two issues have arisen: the handicap of the man and the requirements of the sabbath. The religious leaders saw keeping the sabbath, in accord with their tradition and interpretation, as an inherent part of their faithfulness to God. Jesus addresses the two issues with one question. He calls the handicapped man to stand in front of everyone and then asks the leaders whether "it is lawful to do good on the sabbath rather than to do evil, to save life rather than to destroy it" (3:4).

For Jesus, this situation has implications not only about healing and the sabbath; more pressingly, it involves the very image people have of God. On the assumptions placed before Jesus, God has set up a system that would prevent good being done to someone who needed help. Jesus, in his almost indirect healing of this man, overturns those assumptions. One cannot, Jesus says in effect, imagine a God who would not want to free someone whenever that person needed freedom. One cannot imagine a God who would keep us stuck. God's being involves opening futures for people who think their future is closed.

After Jesus has made clear how the religious leaders have gotten themselves stuck, the passage underlines just how Jesus felt about this. "Looking around at them with anger and grieved at their hardness of heart" (Mark 3:5), Jesus simply asks the man to show his hand to the gathering. The hand is now restored! The agency behind this restoration seems deliberately blurred: Who did the healing? Was it Jesus himself? Did his Father do it behind everyone's back? Did Jesus know what his Father had already done? It makes no difference. Jesus has demonstrated the kind of God that has been revealed throughout Jewish history, even if some emphases of that history had come to blur that revelation. God liberates. God sets free. This God healed in and through Jesus.

Despite all those others with withered limbs, and many with other bodily damage, who did not have the chance to step into the presence of Jesus, this miracle shows what God wants for everyone whose life is limited and impeded in some way. There is a fullness that God wills for us. That invitation comes in many forms, sometimes even in the form of a Messiah wandering around the synagogues of Galilee; often, though, in other ways to which Jesus can open our eyes.

Healing may not always be a cure or correction of a malady, but healing always involves freeing people from the way life has trapped them or even from the ways religious assumptions have trapped them as well. This liberation from what holds people back points directly toward an unlimited future of life.

Forgiveness

Forgiveness, like healing, is a form of liberation. For if people can be held back by their physical and mental limitations, they can also be held back by the patterns of life they have evolved over the years. The Gospel of Matthew shows forgiveness in action for the one who is considered the writer of this Gospel: God calls and forgives Matthew and his associates.

Jesus's encounter with Matthew seems out of the blue. "As Jesus passed on from there, he saw a man named Matthew sitting at the customs post. He said to him,

'Follow me.' And he got up and followed him" (Matt 9:9). Readers cannot skip over the background of this story, for behind this one sentence lies a whole sociology of class and stratification that this one sentence exposes. The gathering at the house of Matthew reveals the complexities that entwined Matthew and his associates.

Tax collectors were categorized with other socially stigmatized sinners, particularly prostitutes. Society indeed regularly stigmatizes and classifies particular groups as evil. But the evil of tax collectors extended far more than their individual decisions to take up this way of making a living. Their very way of life came about through the occupation of Roman authorities over the Jewish people. Unlike the Greeks who saw occupation as a way to extend culture and language, Rome had only one objective: people could keep their culture and language so long as they paid tribute, tax, to Rome. How did they get those taxes? Through tax collectors, of course.

In this way, tax collectors served as traitors to the Jewish people. They worked on behalf of a foreign occupier to exact money from people who, it is clear from the Gospel, did not have much money. To exacerbate this betrayal even more, they often added extra to the amount they claimed was owed, keeping the difference for themselves. One can barely begin to imagine what would make someone undertake this way of life with the result that they had to live on the very edges of the Jewish social world. One can easily imagine, on the other hand, how difficult it would be to get out of this social class, to give up being a tax collector. Once one became a professional cheater and extortioner, how did one return to normal life? It's like leaving a gang or the Mafia; just try it.

At no point in this passage does Jesus say to Matthew (called Levi in other Gospel accounts), "I forgive you. God forgives you. Everything is now fine." Rather, Jesus mingles Matthew's change, his *metanoia* and transformation, with an invitation to a new way of life. "Follow me." Once Matthew does, he immediately begins to leave one social spot and enter another, that of disciple. He moves from one community into another. When Jesus offers reconciliation to Matthew, he is looking to also reconcile different elements of society.

This becomes evident in the scene immediately following Matthew's calling. Jesus is sitting in Matthew's house eating with his tax collector associates; they approached Jesus because of Jesus's breakthrough gesture toward Matthew. The reaction of the Pharisees highlights exactly what is going on: "Why," they ask, "does your teacher eat with tax collectors and sinners?" (Matt 9:11). Groups that are estranged from each other need to stay estranged, right? Otherwise, the lines blur; otherwise, you cannot tell the good from the bad, the righteous from the sinner. Jesus, insisting that his ministry (Kingdom ministry!) is for the hurting and sinners, says to his accusers, "Go and learn the meaning of the words, 'I desire mercy, not sacrifice'" (9:13).

Sacrifice speaks ritual language; mercy speaks relational language. Jesus opens possibilities for sinners, for those seen on the edge of decency, because he opens relationships for them to explore and new identities for them to assume. Who knows how many of Matthew's friends in some way responded to Jesus? The point is that Jesus gave them a chance. "I did not come to call the righteous but sinners," Jesus says (Matt 9:13). Forgiveness, even offered again and again ("seventy times seven") to the point of foolishness, remains the only way for people to respond to the call to change, to connect, to belong once again.

Forgiveness also means entering into a new life and a new world. Our first gut impression leads us to think of it as a way to blot out the past, to not have to carry a burden that seems unbearable. But blotting out a past will work only if someone enters into a new set of relationships, relationships that redefine and support the person in his or her change. For this reason, reconciliation has always been celebrated as a social reality in Christian life. Reconciliation involves God, an individual, and the community in which the individual lives. Moving beyond one's past, the repentant sinner now moves into a community that celebrates union with God through Jesus. Repentance means moving into a new future, one supported by others who also share that future. Forgiveness gives permission for someone to move forward toward something new.

Inclusion

There must be a subtle need for societies to form divisions in which some folks are "in" and others are "out," some are called "good" and others "sinners," some people belong and others are excluded. The greatest instance in our American experience was the practice of slavery accepted for many centuries on American soil and still bearing the fruit of personal and social dislocation 150 years after slavery ended. Every action of Jesus strikes against this social tendency; the deeds by which Jesus enacts the Kingdom, by which he lets the wine of divine joy overflow so as to slake the thirst of everyone, aim to include those previously outlawed or alienated.

Christians, indeed, would reach out to Samaritans and Greeks, to all kinds of foreigners, forming a community that pointed to the universal inclusion that the Kingdom of God envisioned. But this was no easy trick to pull off. The tensions behind this Christian perspective of accepting and including become starkly clear when a Syrophoenician woman approaches Jesus. Mark gives us a scene where Jesus, looking for a break, goes into a house in the district of Tyre; this would have been the area where, historically, Jewish enemies from the west, near the Mediterranean Sea, had come from, the infamous Philistines against whom David gained fame (cf. 1 Sam 17).

She asks Jesus for a healing for her daughter. Shockingly, Jesus appears quite ungracious. "For it is not right to take the food of the children and throw it to the dogs," Jesus says (Mark 7:27), implying that his ministry is more properly for his Jewish compatriots and that non-Jews were like dogs. We can easily surmise the alienation and social distance implied in this remark of Jesus. The usually open and loving Jesus seems quite petulant and even dismissive. But the woman comes back at Jesus: "Lord, even the dogs under the table eat the children's scraps" (Mark 7:28). In other words, one cannot draw sharp lines when it comes to human interchange; neither can such lines be drawn when dealing with God. When slaves mingle with masters, even then there is an interchange!

The woman's faith has crossed a social breach that even Jesus appears to have presumed. No one can be excluded from the mercy God would show. God chooses people not for themselves but as signs of God's broader choice of others. When God chose Abraham, the reason was the ultimate blessing of all nations; "All families of the earth will find blessing in you" (Gen 12:3). No king, prophet, or priest was ever chosen for his own sake; they were chosen to serve others. The actions of Jesus laid a path that his followers would pursue in ways no one could have imagined at first: building a community without the barriers of race or nationality, of class or position. This foreign woman represents every person somehow excluded from "the chosen," or "the pure," or "the correct." As this woman begs for the scraps the supposed children leave behind, so Jesus reveals a boundless scope for those whose faith allows them to smash unfounded barriers. All are children in God's family.

Undoubtedly this story was remembered by the early followers of Jesus precisely for its importance to subsequent church life. All different kinds and classes of people were drawn to the early communities of Christians. Conflicts would be socially unavoidable. Christians would remember how the faith of this foreign woman altered the very terms of the conversation.

~ • ~

Political correctness held little sway when I grew up in the supposedly ideal 1950s. We had slang ways to refer to certain parts of our city and derogatory terms to refer to different kinds of people. Nevertheless, our elevators, stairwells, schools, and subways forced us together into a reality beyond the categories we set up. "Oh, sure, he's Italian," people might say, noting the difference with a smile. "Oh, sure, a Polish girl. How do you spell that name again?" I absorbed, of course, the assumptions of this world of categories and metaphorical boxes; my life of faith, bringing me to encounter others in the love of Christ, keeps crushing those categories and stereotypes. Subsequent history has taught us how easy it is to use suspicions and differences to deepen divisions, often for political (and therefore economic) benefit.

Perhaps no facet of the Kingdom seems more difficult than the signs by which the Kingdom—in its breadth and comprehensive scope—are enacted in ways that make a claim on the imagination, and conscience, of every person. Churches continue to need to relearn lessons of inclusion because they can so easily use social status as a crutch to organize themselves.

As a Church, a community of disciples who follow Jesus, obedience to the liberating aspects of the Kingdom have come often with great difficulty. Whether with the Church's blessing or without it, barriers, obstacles, and denunciation have sprung up regularly throughout Christian history.

The Kingdom, as the Second Vatican Council taught, subsists in the Church; but dimensions of the Kingdom spill over beyond the Church, a universal grace and mercy of which the Church is the Sacrament but not the exclusive possessor. Christ assumed our flesh; therefore, he assumed all human flesh. His Body, the Church, becomes truest to its purpose when healing, forgiveness, and inclusion stand out as its actions.

What barriers do we inadvertently erect? What barriers are waiting for demolition? Jesus's signs of the Kingdom keep drawing big pictures for us to see.

Meditation: Progress

Although the modern world doesn't think of itself as very consciously religious, that might not be totally true. When we think of the ideals that Jesus espoused—of healing, forgiveness, and inclusion—in some ways these have become the goals of a lot of modern searching. Certainly, we have come to think of medicine as an almost assured means of healing. In fact, when someone is not healed, medical professionals feel they have to come up with some technical explanation.

The work of social and mental health workers, too, certainly stems from a desire to help people find reconciliation. Perhaps that means reconciliation with oneself through patterns of therapy in which the fissures of one's past might be fused together into a new pattern of living. It might also mean reconciliation between various social sectors, particularly when they are racially charged. Indeed, do not many politicians get their start by seeming to offer a way to bring society to a new level of unity?

Perhaps no force has been greater than the media to bring about greater inclusion. Through news reporting of other countries and cultures, through diversifying the kinds of people playing in sports or in various fictional stories, people have their eyes opened. Yes, a black man can play baseball! Yes, a woman can run a company! Yes, families do exist that seem different than the one I grew up in! Yes, gay and lesbian people do seem able to be faithfully committed!

It is easy to dismiss the "myth of progress" in which we can naively assume that everything is moving forward and making things better. The very technological progress we have made, applied to weapons or even financial markets, can bring about destruction and economic depression far more extensive than at any other point in human history. Warriors can throw spears, but dropping cluster bombs raises the stakes unimaginably.

But we dismiss whole aspects of the desire for progress at our own risk. Progress, at the very least, wants to alleviate the built-in destructive forces of human nature: the hurt, the divisions, the inequalities, the death. In this way, modern progress has assumed, to a large extent, the mantle of Jesus. Religious thinkers will say, right away,

DISCIPLESHIP FOR THE FUTURE

that we do not bring the Kingdom; it is God's gift to us. But that gift, of itself, engenders actions that spring from a dream of greater wholeness for humankind.

Modern progress is certainly not religion. But that doesn't mean it doesn't have religious roots and impulses.

Can it be that all the study of the material world, of the earth and its environment, of the human person's body and mind, of our planet and our planetary system, might actually make more sense if it is viewed not in opposition to faith but as an outgrowth of faith—at least faith in the Kingdom? Can it be that science and faith might be much closer to each other than people often make it look on paper?

Can one of Jesus's miracles be the way his life inspired so many ideals pursued by science, in the hope of making life less wretched and more complete?

~ • ~

For Reflection and Discussion

Read the following passage slowly and thoughtfully.

Luke 9:1-6

He summoned the Twelve and gave them power and authority over all demons and to cure diseases, and he sent them to proclaim the kingdom of God and to heal [the sick]. He said to them, "Take nothing for the journey, neither walking stick, nor sack, nor food, nor money, and let no one take a second tunic. Whatever house you enter, stay there and leave from there. And as for those who do not welcome you, when you leave that town, shake the dust from your feet in testimony against them." Then they set out and went from village to village proclaiming the good news and curing diseases everywhere.

1. What kinds of reaction would you have if Jesus had asked you to accompany this group of twelve apostles? How might they be like the feelings of the apostles back then?
2. What does Jesus ask his disciples to do as a sign of the Kingdom? What might be something equivalent Jesus is asking of his followers today?
3. Jesus's method was to be direct and keep it simple: "Take nothing for the journey," he says. What are the most direct and simple actions you see Christians doing today that might help people see what his good news is about?

Slowly pray the Lord's Prayer and conclude by asking God's blessing on you and yours.

Chapter 4

THE LOGIC
OF THE KINGDOM

SOME OPERAS AND MANY Broadway shows begin with an extended playing of music that contains the main themes one will hear in the ensuing production. These warm up the audience for what to expect. Many books also begin with introductions that try to synthesize the main arguments or insights of the book to get the reader on board from the beginning.

Americans are used to hearing the opening of the Declaration of Independence as a way to put out the political project that began the United States of America: "We hold these truths to be self-evident, that all men are created equal, that they are endowed by their Creator with certain unalienable Rights, that among these are Life, Liberty and the pursuit of Happiness." We can feel a certain spirit in these words that supports the ongoing vision of what we think America stands for.

Christian faith has something like this in the major teachings of Jesus. These teachings are preserved in different ways in the Gospels of Matthew and Luke. Matthew, speaking to a Jewish Christian audience, uses the imagery of Moses, the teacher of God's law, to frame the teaching of Jesus. As Moses went up Mt. Sinai to receive the teachings of God, so the disciples gather around Jesus on a high mountain to hear him present God's teachings for his disciples. Luke has Jesus teaching on a plain, but the source material for each account is the same.

Jesus, in what we call the Sermon on the Mount (chapters 5—7 of Matthew's Gospel), gives a prologue to the rest of the Gospel, highlighting those assumptions, attitudes, and behaviors that compose the spirituality of his disciples. All of Jesus's teaching in this part of the Gospel finds its orientation in the proclamation of the Kingdom. Here Jesus gives the "logic" of the Kingdom— what makes it tick and what makes it work for those who would belong to it. The logic of Jesus's teaching reinforces the mentality of conversion to which his disciples were invited when Jesus first proclaimed the Kingdom.

As with everything that has to do with the Kingdom, this logic bears down both on immediate experience and on our ultimate anticipations of fulfillment, creating that tension out of which springs a vision of today that looks toward tomorrow, toward the future.

Beatitude

Jesus opens the Sermon on the Mount with a series of sayings in which he declares certain kinds of people to be "blessed." We call this list the "Beatitudes," a name that comes from the Latin word for "blessed"—*beatus*. While this word is at times translated as "happy," it does not have the sense of happiness that, say, going to a party or going to a theme park might carry. In fact, the actual phrasings imply just the opposite. For Jesus declares people happy that many of us today might think of as particularly unfortunate and miserable. After all, he begins with a statement that shocks us: "Blessed are the poor...."

The irony of calling happy those whom many would consider unfortunate reveals the paradox behind Jesus's teachings. The seeming contradiction of his words forces us to deeper considerations of his teaching. It forces us to grapple with the logic of the Kingdom that Jesus is revealing, a logic that, while seeming counterintuitive at first, ultimately makes compelling sense. The logic, ultimately, ties present to future, time to eternity.

When we look at the Beatitudes in the opening lines of chapter 5 of Matthew's Gospel, we immediately note they have a structure; the first three refer to attitudes, while the remainder refer to actions. When we think about it, the list of Ten Commandments has a similar structure, with the first three referring to our relationship to God and the remaining seven commandments referring to how we relate to each other. Each Beatitude adds an image to the ultimate vision of the Kingdom, showing us what the fullness of life and love might look like from the perspective of God.

How paradoxical, even contradictory, it seems to call blessed and happy those who are poor, who weep, and who are lowly! These people are said to receive unqualified blessings. These are the ones who will receive comfort, inherit the land, and already possess the Kingdom. Jesus speaks of the Kingdom as something already possessed and as something yet to come, building that dynamic tension that pitches time forward toward fulfillment. The paradox of Jesus's words comes from the perspective he assumes: people who have a vision of the Kingdom, when God's love holds sway and brings everything into fulfillment, grasp our present moments differently than those who do not.

The paradox can be resolved only by understanding that people who ground their lives in their possessions, their own joy, or their status have placed their reliance on what is other and less than God. They presume to hold control over their lives by their efforts. Instead of living in complete trust in God, their trust jumps from one desperate grasp to another, in a fickle attempt to secure their own lives. We only need to look at the frenzy often behind our financial markets to see this. When one is freed from this desperate grasping, then one has found the beatitude that can only come from radical trust in God.

This opens up the logic of the Kingdom: the happiness that comes from our total trust in a God of infinite love and life then frees us to share happiness with all the others God sends into our lives. Freedom to serve and live for others, and the future, characterizes the disciples of Jesus.

As a result of a new relationship with God, our Father, we can then hunger and work for justice; we can then extend mercy to others; we can live with integrity toward God and others; we can work for peace; we can even face persecution and attacks. To these people belong the Kingdom of God. All of this is a gradually deeper vision that clarifies the God in whom we have placed our trust, the mercy we will receive, and the status we have as God's children.

Haven't we met, at times, people who seem totally free? There is a story about an Argentine golfer, Roberto de Vincenzo, who was approached by a woman at the end of a golf tournament. She had a story of desperation: her child was dying, and she had no resources to pay for the care the child needed. Roberto endorsed the check with his winnings and gave it to her. The following week, after word had gotten around, he was approached by some who told him that he was scammed by the woman. He replied, "You mean there was no emergency, no dying child, no desperate mother?" He paused, looked around and then said, "That's the best news I've heard all week." How can we be free enough to let go of our need to have, to control, to win?

At every point in Jesus's life and teaching, this relationship of loving trust with the Father is the foundation of everything. Jesus not only teaches this; he lives it in his ministry, even to the moments of his agony and death. Believers should be able to see this woven through their faith actions. Every reception of a sacrament means committing oneself more deeply in loving trust to God. Every reading of the Scripture calls for this loving trust. Every action we do to serve others flows not only from our good-hearted generosity but, more deeply, from the utter trust we have come to have in God.

Prayer

Once Jesus has elaborated the logic of the Kingdom, he proceeds to apply this to various dimensions of the lives of his followers. Prayer is one of those dimensions. In the Sermon on the Mount, Jesus touches on prayer in two particular ways. First, he talks about how and for whom we are to pray. Second, he gives us a prayer to recite, one that parallels the Beatitudes in a remarkable way.

The context for Jesus's teaching on prayer comes near the end of chapter 6 of Matthew's Gospel when Jesus asks people to look at their basic attitude of trust. "Therefore I tell you, do not worry about your life, what you will eat [or drink], or about your body, what you will wear" (Matt 6:25). Again, given the amount of advertising we absorb today that ramps up worries precisely in these areas, Jesus's statement seems totally countercultural. Just as we are puzzled when he pronounces the poor and humble to be blessed, so we are astounded when Jesus asks us not to worry about the very things that we spend most of our time worrying about.

Beyond the observation that most of human worry is a waste of energy, Jesus asks us to take a good look at the overwhelming richness of our very existence—including the generous care that lies behind everything. Can we not see the beauty and splendor of the grass on which we walk, or the way birds seem to take care of themselves almost without effort? "Can any of you by worrying add a single moment to your life-span?" (Matt 6:27). If God provides for the world we see around us with a loving generosity evidenced everywhere, "will he not much more provide for you, O you of little faith?" (Matt 6:30). Again, Jesus invites us to the foundational core of our experience of life, which is, at the same time, the basis of our foundational trust in God.

The effect that science had on Christian imagination when the Industrial Revolution began has been called "disenchantment." Instead of seeing angels and saints and God's loving hand, thinkers saw immutable laws of physics that applied causality irrespective of people or their concerns. The world lost its magic, lost its personalism. Humans seemed to be an anomaly, sensitive and sentient beings in an otherwise cold and colorless universe. Jesus invites us to question this disenchantment for one clear reason: we can sense a love and care far exceeding the workings of a machine. We can sense, and build our lives on, a world of warmth and grace. Rather than being depersonalized, existence is hyper-personalized because love can be seen, in some way, anywhere we look.

This radical trust that Jesus opens for us shows itself in the first lines of the prayer that he taught his disciples:

Our Father in heaven,
    hallowed be your name,
    your kingdom come,
    your will be done,
       on earth as in heaven. (Matt 6:9–10)

We have a God in common with each other and with all the universe; we understand this God as "Father." Before we apply the appropriate sensitivities that feminist thinking has taught us, before we dismiss the word *Father*, we need to see how it would have resonated in the culture of Jesus. *Father* meant a boundless source of loving care, the very opposite of the "forces" and "laws" that many imagine structure their lives. Because God is this unlimited source of love and care, God's name, God's very reality, is deemed to be holy, sacred, and beyond profanation. In other words, we can treat nothing else in our experience the way we treat this God of infinite love. *Father* ultimately serves as a metaphor for the caring love we experience in our lives.

And what is God about? What does God want? This prayer tells us, God's will is to bring about God's Kingdom. This Kingdom happens when God's unbounded love has no opposition, no distortion, no dismissal. The Kingdom happens when God's will for the fullness of life and love spans all of existence, earth and heaven. As in the Beatitudes, once we are clear about on whom we depend and why, there ensues a freedom expressed in the generous love we show others.

Give us today our daily bread;
and forgive us our debts,
as we forgive our debtors;
and do not subject us to the final test,
but deliver us from the evil one.
(Matt 6:11–13)

According to the way the Kingdom works, once we have clear God's relationship with us, and our relation to God, then we can freely give of ourselves because God has assured us despite our fundamental insecurity. "If you then, who are wicked, know how to give good gifts to your children, how much more will your heavenly Father give good things to those who ask him" (Matt 7:11).

In the Lord's prayer we notice two needs that seem, at first, unconnected: our need for bread and our need to forgive. The God who feeds the birds of the air will feed us "our daily bread"—which means the immediate needs we have rather than the excessive needs we imagine we have. Bread for today, for the work and ministry we are called to do, for the company of family and friends—this God provides. (And, in times of famine, God provides through the way we provide for each other.) We need our "daily bread" and are astonished at how readily it is given.

But we need forgiveness in the same way we need bread because our refusal to forgive closes us off to the very world of merciful grace on which we all depend. We are forgiven as we forgive because, until we forgive, we do not even know what forgiveness is. The freedom that allows us to let go of our resentments and grudges also lets us see the abundant love God freely pours upon the world.

This means that foundational trust in God also gives us insight into the priority of God's mercy. God extends a healing and reconciling hand toward us blundering humans as soon as the wound of our sins appears. Mercy, like divine love, is not some almost impossible gift that we must beg for; indeed, mercy stands at the heart of our relationship with God because we encounter a God that heals and forgives by God's very nature. A spirituality of the Kingdom sees mercy as the starting point of God's involvement with us because mercy, uniquely, opens up a future that would otherwise be blocked.

How people, on the basis of saving face, can allow estrangement to continue for years, each demanding some sign that she or he was "right," shows how our petty ideas about justice can box us in to rigid positions that, ultimately, serve no purpose. When we exercise mercy, that is, take the initiative of showing reconciliation and openness to another, things begin to change; movement becomes possible. Nelson Mandela taught this vigorously to his peers: he knew that unless he forgave, he would never really be released from the prisons of South Africa that held him captive for twenty-seven years. So long as he could not find in his heart the ability to forgive those who resisted him, he would remain, metaphorically, trapped in prison.

Instead of imposing our standards of "justice" in the form of getting even and feeling revenge onto God, Christians should see what language Jesus uses of his Father and enter into the mystery of mercy that allows insight into the kind of love God is and offers. "Justice," as the making right of everything, comes as the ultimate gift of mercy. Justice looks to correct a past that ultimately cannot be deleted; mercy looks to open a future filled with unthought possibilities.

The radical trust we have in God also sustains us through the end. This is what the final petition of the Our Father concerns, namely, how our trust in God allows us to remain faithful through all the tests that we face. Pope Francis has questioned the translation "lead us not into temptation," because it implies that God tempts us, something a good God would not do. But the original sense of the language is something like this: do not let us be subjected to the final trials of the end-times; protect us from the very source of evil. That we pray this every day indicates that the testing of the final days is not entirely different from the testing that we all daily undergo. What is that test? Precisely to trust, or not, in the Father's love.

The act of praying, with its total trust and openness, changes the world in which we live. We most frequently think of prayer as petition, a praying for something. But Jesus's prayer shows how our praying orients us to a final vision of life. Prayer directs us to the God of love, but this God of love opens for us possibilities for our lives, possibilities that we have often blocked out through cynicism or anger. The whole of existence, present and future, unfolds in our lives when we stand before God in trust. When we can even face potential final days of trial, we can, by that very reason, face the future God is always opening for us.

When we pray, we align our wills with God's will: we pray for the Kingdom.

Prayer is fundamental to all spirituality because it changes the context of our lives. Prayer opens our vision to possibilities that we otherwise could not see. We shape our thinking to the potentialities of our own efforts, to the possibilities that culture sets out for us. "Oh, that's not going to happen," we shrug. As a result, we shrink what we think our future can be. Jesus's "miracles," the acts that flowed from his prayer, were primarily the possibilities that others doubted but he could see. Without prayer, we cannot see even the possibility of change; we cannot see the openness the future should have.

Prayer connects the various layers that make up our existence, opening up for us layers of love and power that we routinely dismiss. Our eyes seem most comfortable with the usual, the normal, the predictable. We cannot easily see all the possibilities, all the possible futures, that can happen. But prayer shapes our lives in a way that allows what seems, to us, least likely and most impossible, as another way things might come about. For the layer that enwraps all the others is that of divine love. This layer prayer opens for us in a way like no other.

Love

Jesus also speaks about love, showing us that it flows from the basic pattern of radical trust in God that opens us toward God's future. God's love, universal and unrestricted, becomes the pattern for the actions of all of Christ's disciples. Do we not have a heavenly Father who "makes his sun rise on the bad and the good, and causes rain to fall on the just and the unjust" (Matt 5:45)? How can we be children of this kind of Father without having the same expansive love that God shows? Jesus, the Son of this Father in heaven, reflects this love in everything he does. We become God's daughters and sons by our sharing in Jesus's relationship with his Father.

Jesus proceeds further with the demands of love. "For if you love those who love you, what recompense will you have? Do not tax collectors do the same?" (Matt 5:46). We cannot reduce God's love to the instinctual belongings of family or the preferential choices of those whom we come to like. God's love, expansive and encompassing, remains the standard for all human interaction.

As we think about this, we realize just how future directed this ideal of love is. When, after all, will we love as the Father loves? Does this not remain a challenge and goal that pulls us ever forward toward something greater? In one exchange Jesus had with a scribe who asked him the greatest commandment, they both come to affirm what Jesus lays out: "He said to him, 'You shall love the Lord, your God, with all your heart, with all your soul, and with all your mind. This is the greatest and the first commandment. The second is like it: You shall love your neighbor as yourself'" (Matt 22:37–39).

Jesus's words on love reference some of the most central texts of Jewish revelation, from the ancient books of Leviticus and Deuteronomy. But few words capture the very tension we have been pointing to in our study of discipleship and the Kingdom as do these. They point to the present, of course, showing how we are to act. But they also point to the future because they cannot be completely accomplished in our own life span. When will we have loved God with all our heart or soul? When will we have reached "all" of our mind and soul? Only when we attain a completeness toward which every moment of our lives is tending. Only when the Kingdom, for which we all seek and serve, comes in its completeness.

If we imagine the Kingdom as that state in which we have come to full love—loving God with all that is within us, loving others as we love ourselves—we then realize heaven can be no static place, as if it were a painting or mathematical formula that was "complete." The final state of the Kingdom can only be conceived as the dynamic activation of our relationships with others and with God, an activation in which we stand unendingly toward the other, beyond ourselves, in love. The nature of the Kingdom as a reality of transformed relationship becomes undeniable with Jesus's vision of love. Beatitude means giving ourselves to the other, for the sake of the other, in complete joy, because God has given everything to us in love.

The logic of love completes the logic of prayer and that of blessedness.

~ • ~

The logic of the Kingdom is our anticipation of its fullness through our relationship with a God who is a father of unbounded love. This glimpse, this peek, grounds the trust we need to get beyond our insecurity and stinginess. It opens us up to a freedom that transforms all our moments by allowing them to be other-directed and future-directed. The Kingdom creates a horizon for us, an encompassing goal that we cannot exhaust ourselves. Our love and service toward that goal grounds the substance of our discipleship as followers of Jesus in pursuit of the Kingdom he inaugurates.

Meditation: Reconciliation and Love

I frequently imagine the Easter event told in John's Gospel (ch. 21). I see the disciples out on their familiar boats in their very familiar lake, trying to catch fish. I wonder how it is that, after experiencing the life, death, and resurrection of Jesus, they can go back to what they had always done, that catching fish would be enough.

Jesus is on shore cooking fish—the very fish the disciples want to catch but seemingly cannot. "Throw your nets over the other side," Jesus calls to the disciples who, going about daily work, barely recognize him. Only when their nets swell with fish does it dawn on Peter that "it is the Lord." We feel his confused excitement as he rearranges his clothes and jumps into the water, swimming toward the one he denied.

As they drag in the dozens of large fish that they caught—fish that seemed impossible to catch just a few minutes before—Jesus invites them to a meal. "Sit down with me and be one with me. Share your hopes and lives with me." Now they have leisure time with Jesus, time to study his risen form, time to pass scraps of fish between themselves and Jesus.

What was going on in their minds? Was Jesus showing them that even their old lives as fishermen could be enchanted? That his glory is accessible in every life now that he has been raised? Or was he offering them a kind of reconciliation, a chance to go beyond their fleeing of betrayal when they abandoned Jesus in their fear? Was Jesus healing up wounds so that they could heal the wounds of others?

"Simon, son of John." Jesus calls Peter by his original name, not the one Jesus had given him earlier. Peter did not understand what it meant to be named "Rock" by Jesus. Maybe Jesus is trying again....

"Do you love me more than these?" What is Jesus asking? It is not about some emotional state in Peter's consciousness. "More than these" has to refer to the other disciples. Was Peter willing to give himself in trust to the mission of Jesus, even if it would cost him more than what it would cost the other disciples? Was there a limit to Peter's love? "Lord, you know everything, you know that I love you," Peter says in summary.

"Feed my lambs. Tend my sheep." In other words, Peter shows his love of Jesus by the loving service he would

show others. Coming to trust in Jesus need not amount principally to more or deeper words. But it had to amount to greater care for others, greater giving of oneself, greater sacrifice...even if that would entail Peter giving his life, one day, as a sign of total trust. Peter's reconciliation came from a renewed encounter of Jesus and his mercy.

A renewed encounter toward which everyone can be open. A renewed encounter in trust that makes even death a stepping-stone to something more, a stepping-stone into the future.

"Follow me," says Jesus. And Peter does.

~ • ~

For Reflection and Discussion

Read this passage slowly and thoughtfully.

Matthew 6:25–30

Therefore I tell you, do not worry about your life, what you will eat [or drink], or about your body, what you will wear. Is not life more than food and the body more than clothing? Look at the birds in the sky; they do not sow or reap, they gather nothing into barns, yet your heavenly Father feeds them. Are not you more important than they? Can any of you by worrying add a single moment to your life-span? Why are you anxious about clothes? Learn from the way the wild flowers grow. They do not work or spin. But I tell you that not even Solomon in all his splendor was clothed like one of them. If God so clothes the grass of the field, which grows today and is thrown into the oven tomorrow, will he not much more provide for you, O you of little faith?

1. As you listen to these words of Jesus, which of them seem easier or harder for you to hear and accept?
2. Think of moments in your life that forced you to have great trust in God. What were they like?
3. In our modern world of markets and economic theory, does Jesus's attitude have anything to offer people today?

Slowly pray the Lord's Prayer and conclude by asking God's blessing on you and yours.

Chapter 5

IMAGINING THE KINGDOM

I'M THE KIND OF PERSON Ikea may not like. I can look at an item in the store; I can purchase the parts and put them on the floor; I can even lay out all the screws and hinges. But I cannot follow the directions. The directions will contain a word as if everyone knew immediately what that word meant (not to mention that the directions seem to have been translated into their third language). What do they mean by "flange"? What kind of screw are they talking about?

Well, people might say, just go on YouTube and you'll surely find someone putting the very item together; just follow the pictures. Indeed, the pictures are what I need. Not everyone can think in three-dimensional terms. But will I put in the ten minutes the video is asking of me? Arrogant and self-assured, I'll stick to the directions, forcing pieces of the furniture together, like the stereotypical male driver refusing to stop at the gas station to ask for help when lost.

I'm too proud to admit that, in the end, I need a picture.

For some people, pictures come easily. They can generate images both visual and verbal on the spot. Others, like me, live in a flatter world in which we expect everything to be self-explanatory. What an assumption to make, however: that everything would be self-explanatory. Every moment of our lives is a boundless mystery—not in the sense of an unsolvable puzzle but more in the sense of an excess of being and meaning.

When reality is like this, the only thing that works are images that point beyond themselves to the mystery of love that surrounds us.

~ • ~

Can you draw me a picture of the Kingdom?

For all that Jesus talked about the Kingdom, his words basically pointed to the kinds of behaviors his followers needed to have in order to belong to the Kingdom. In other words, the Kingdom is something that you see through what you are doing and through the attitudes you have developed in relation to the Kingdom. We know the Kingdom more through behavior than theorizing; indeed, we can only think about the Kingdom by reflecting on our actions. Rather than develop a theology or produce a philosophy of the Kingdom, Jesus told stories and created images.

"Here," he says in effect, "tell me what this story does to your heart and mind!" For the images that Jesus creates, the stories he tells, evoke surprise and puzzlement, pushing in several directions at the same time.

Where do we find ourselves in these stories? How do they define us; how do they push us out of our comfort zones?

We find Jesus's parables mostly in the Gospels of Matthew, Mark, and Luke. Luke has parables that the other Gospels do not, notably the Good Samaritan and the Prodigal Son. That the Gospels present these parables so predominantly to us shows the part they played in the lives of the early followers of Jesus. We have to imagine those first disciples sitting around, teasing out the different aspects of the image and applying the images to their own lives as individuals and as communities. In this sense, a parable does not necessarily have one clear meaning; the meaning, rather, is found in how they are applied.

Should we not join with them? Should we not see what the stories do for us? In the examples of parables below, it makes no sense to repeat the parable, one after another, although both Mark and Matthew have collections of parables edited together. Rather, read the parable, let it do what it will do to you (shock, surprise, puzzle, discomfit), and use the questions to apply them to your own life.

~ • ~

Matthew and Mark

The sower throws seed here and there, letting it fall in many places; a lot of it is wasted but some of it bears fruit (Mark 4:1ff.; Matt 13:1ff.).

- How many false starts and half-intentions are in our own lives?
- What makes some seed fall where it can bear fruit?
- How much fruit is God's Word bearing in my own life?
- How frail, yet how substantial, is this Kingdom of Jesus!

We know what to do with a lamp. We know it's purpose. You let its light shine (Mark 4:21ff.; Matt 6:14). Why would you ever put it under the bed or under a basket?

* How has light shone in my own life?
* How do I reflect God's light to others?
* How do I obscure the light that God has given me?
* On whom is God asking that light shine through me?

We plant things and they grow. Sometimes we are surprised at what grows from what we sow. The growth happens whether we can see it or not, almost automatically. How fruitful might the Kingdom be if we do not impede its growth (see Mark 4:26ff.; Matt 13:31ff.)?

* How have I been surprised at what the gospel has caused to grow in my life?
* Have I lived with mistrust in the power of God in my life?
* How is what grows in me helping others?
* How sacred is our earth, that so much can come from it! But how easily it can be damaged.
* Do I trust the Kingdom to grow? Do I need to control the Kingdom? Can I rejoice in its growth?

Perhaps our gardens cannot be perfect. Who judges the imperfection? God's goals and vision are more important than ours. Sometimes weeds and wheat grow together. Do we trust the wheat to still flourish (Matt

13:24ff.)? Similarly, Jesus talks about those who think their houses are perfectly clean (Matt 12:43–45).

- How often do I insist that I know best?
- What does my judgmentalism do to the lives of others?
- Do I trust what God is doing in my life? Do I trust what God may be doing in the lives of others?
- What price do we pay for the illusion of our perfection?
- What does pride do to my ability to live in Christ's Kingdom?

The Kingdom does not come to those who have no ambition, who let opportunities slip away, who do not sacrifice because they do not believe in the importance of the Kingdom. If you want it, go for it (Matt 13:44ff.; Luke 19:12ff.)!

- We know what we have to do but keep putting it off.
- I'm not willing to pay the price even though it means everything to me.
- Why can't I just sit around and watch?
- Am I doing this basically for myself? Or is it for others and for God?
- How important is the Kingdom to me?

You cannot let up, even when things get difficult. Faithfulness is essential to the Kingdom. This means being generous and hardworking for God all the way until the end (Matt 20:1ff.; 22:1ff.; 25:2ff.; 25:14ff.).

- How often do self-pity and self-absorption keep me from being focused?
- Do I always think that everything is primarily about me?
- Do I trust that if I am faithful God will be faithful to me?
- Do I resent being a servant?

What do you think judgment will be like? What is it that God ultimately expects of me, of us? God expects us to reflect the mercy and love that God shows to all. Everything is moving toward completion and toward a judgment we cannot avoid (Matt 18:20ff.; 25:31ff.).

- What do I think it will be like to stand before God?
- What about my life really concerns God? What about our lives gets God's interest?
- Do I think I need to be and act toward others as God has been and acted toward me?
- Do I think I will be judged precisely on the issue of mercy?

Luke

Luke has his own way of using parables that parallels Matthew and Mark in that he seems to want to emphasize a particular kind of behavior in the parables he presents. More stories than elaborate metaphors, Luke's parables are among the most memorable. Because the behaviors these parables identify are so gripping, we return to them again and again.

Jesus explains who our neighbors are by telling the story of the Samaritan (and not the priest or Levite) bending down to help the injured Jewish man (Luke 10:25ff.).

- Is the Kingdom truly universal for me? Or is it about my favorites and my preferences?
- Is there a limit I can place on compassion? What does it mean to have compassion for everyone? What must I constantly look out for?
- When have I worried about someone else more than myself?

A man had two sons but the younger one wanted his inheritance immediately; he left his father and brother to dissipate everything that the father had given him. But he returns in desperation and the father makes a big deal out of the young son. "My son was dead but has come back to life." But the older brother resents the treatment his younger brother gets and cannot understand the father's behavior (Luke 15:11ff.).

- How many chances do I think people should get?
- Which brother do I think I am? What does my community think of wrongdoers?
- How much leeway should criminals and prisoners get?
- What is the power of conversion in our lives?
- What makes us resistant to conversion?

~ • ~

We want things nailed down, black and white, with no ambiguities.

Jesus won't let us off that easily.

It's not a question of information that we know; more, it's about an ability to see, to keep on seeing, and to refine the sight that we have.

Some things do not come in an "either-or" package inasmuch as they are insights and attitudes that have to grow over time and sometimes even change their meaning over time. What does faithfulness mean when I am a teenager? Or what does faithfulness mean if I am seventy and riddled with painful cancer? What demands will generosity continue to make on me? What do my actions allow me to see of God's Kingdom? Of God's nature? Of God's love?

Jesus's parables haunt the souls of everyone who hears them. Each of us immediately sees ourselves somewhere in Jesus's images and stories. They gnaw at our consciences; they expand our minds and hearts. They insist we look at what's immediately before us—and also what God's ultimate vision looks like.

We hear these parables as individuals, letting them spur our hearts further forward. Yet we also hear these parables together, as a community. They address our present moments, but they also push upon us, as a community, ideals that demand a common striving. Our communities are the seed that has been sown. We are the field with wheat and weeds. We can be the older brother or the young brother—or we can be the father. Whom do we walk by and how does our common disinterest permit us to ignore the suffering around us? What price do we pay for thinking we are a perfect Church? What are we doing with the gifts that have been given us? For what purpose are these gifts multiplied?

What do we use our energy for? For what's essential and beautiful, or for what's safest and demands the least from us? For what do we think we are answerable? For our lives...our family...our parish community...our neighborhood and neighbors...our country and its basic values...our entire planet...the world's future?

The parables permit no easy answers because they are meant to disquiet us, to keep us alert, to keep us wondering and self-critical. "Whoever has ears ought to hear" (Matt 13:9).

A spirituality for Christ's Kingdom insists that we be alert for the "more" that God keeps promising us and creation.

Meditation: A Modern Parable

He thought he had it all. He was ready for a comfortable life, one lived at his whim and disposal. He could dictate this or that to those around him. "Me first" was his inner slogan.

People would ask things of him. He would think and judge. "I don't like this one. I don't think that one is worthy." His generosity was strangely stingy.

One day he felt a bit unwell. He started asking around. People pointed out to him how many other people felt unwell. "They probably contaminated me!" he grunted.

His nurse attended to his needs as he mumbled and grumbled. "Poor me, they got me sick," he said. She gave him his medications and quietly remarked, "What makes you think you are not connected to them in the first place? That you are separate and untouchable?" He looked at her in puzzlement. "I'm a different kind of person from all of those folks."

"Are you really?" she smiled.

~ • ~

For Reflection and Discussion

Read this passage slowly and thoughtfully.

Matthew 13:24-30

[Jesus] proposed another parable to them. "The kingdom of heaven may be likened to a man who sowed good seed in his field. While everyone was asleep his enemy came and sowed weeds all through the wheat, and then went off. When the crop grew and bore fruit, the weeds appeared as well. The slaves of the householder came to him and said, 'Master, did you not sow good seed in your field? Where have the weeds come from?' He answered, 'An enemy has done this.' His slaves said to him, 'Do you want us to go and pull them up?' He replied, 'No, if you pull up the weeds you might uproot the wheat along with them. Let them grow together until harvest; then at harvest time I will say to the harvesters, "First collect the weeds and tie them in bundles for burning; but gather the wheat into my barn."'"

1. Why do you think Jesus told this parable? At whom might it be aimed?
2. What do you think are the greatest forces sowing "weeds" in modern culture? How would you describe them?
3. What do you think of the optimism of the farmer? Do you feel it might be overstated? What about the attitudes of the slaves?

Slowly pray the Lord's Prayer and conclude by asking God's blessing on you and yours.

Chapter 6

THE GLORY
OF THE KINGDOM

WHAT IS THERE ABOUT new clothes, especially something a bit expensive like a new suit?

As soon as I'd get home with a suit, I'd rush to put it on. A small part is whether the pants would fit, whether the sleeves would be a bit too long, whether I'd have to visit a tailor to have things adjusted. But the bigger part of this exercise is walking to a mirror, as full length as possible, and seeing how the suit makes me look. Does it flatter me? Does it hide how my shoulders tend to slope or how pudgy I've gotten? Will it help me appear impressive to others?

If my new suit makes me feel better about myself, maybe I will in fact be better! Maybe I'll wow them, and they'll pay more attention to me. "You can't make a good impression with a cheap suit," I was told. Clothes sometimes say more than we think.

In ancient Israel, this might have been the function of the cloak, the garment worn on the outside, like the Coat of Many Colors that Jacob had woven for his favorite son, Joseph (Gen 37:3). This would have been much flashier than any suit I might buy; it was so flashy that it reinforced the jealousy of Joseph's brothers against him. I keep remembering, too, that when Jesus was crucified, soldiers threw dice to see who would get his clothes (John 19:23–24; Matt 27:35). As John describes it, it was a tunic of such quality that it could not be torn and divided. I wonder about Jesus's clothes, whether he dressed to stand out, to get the attention of others. Did he get advice on dressing from the men and women who followed him?

A section in the ritual for baptism includes the bestowal of a white robe or gown. The ritual states that the robe is a sign of the newly baptized person's dignity. Its whiteness underscores the innocence of a newly begun life in Christ. "Keep that garment unstained," the ritual says. The gown shows who I am and who I hope to become through the sacrament.

But dressing well might not be just about the individual person, about me. It could be, in a big way, about others too. When people dress up for me, am I not flattered? When clergy put on elegant vestments, does not the congregation sense something about itself? When countries insist their royalty wear certain clothes and don certain crowns, doesn't that affect how the subjects feel about themselves? When we applaud well-dressed celebrities, doesn't that make us feel their glow has come upon us? When people watch the Oscars, are they not looking more at the dresses than listening to the acceptance speeches?

I'm sure this is why Jesus, at least on one occasion, decided to dazzle his followers.

~ • ~

Glory

One of the ways we feel we can anticipate the fullness of the Kingdom is by the experience of glory. Liturgy sometimes provides this sense, particularly on big feasts or celebrations like ordination or marriage. There might be a hymn that gets the whole congregation singing or, more rarely, a homily or sermon of great force. A special event makes us feel special just because we are part of it.

In the first chapter of the Gospel of John we find this statement:

> And the Word became flesh
>   and made his dwelling among us,
>   and we saw his glory,
>   the glory as of the Father's only Son,
>   full of grace and truth. (John 1:14)

Paradoxically, the "glory" that John shows throughout his Gospel is very much connected to the "Word became flesh"—it's the glory of the deeds that Jesus did for people to bring them the saving help they needed and to aid them in seeing what God is like. Among the things of glory that stand out in John's Gospel are the raising of Lazarus and the washing of the disciples' feet. Ultimately, Jesus's glory shines through his crucifixion in which he is "lifted up" in glory (John 12:32, 34). John strives to show God transparently working through the whole life of Jesus, in all his words and deeds. He has less need for the lights and drama we usually associate with glory. To die on the cross, to love to the end, to breathe out his "spirit"—this is Jesus's greatest sign, the fulfillment of all the other signs and wonders that we read about in John's Gospel.

Glory is similar to the idea of miracle that we saw in chapter 3. We noted there that one of the ideas associated with the word *miracle* was "to see" something that struck us. Glory is like that too. When something appears glorious to us, we cannot take our eyes off of it. Do we not often associate glory with theater, musical events, or even movies? Things that move us because of their appeal are called glorious.

The history of the Church shows varying attitudes toward glory, at least in terms of the fabric of our church buildings and their appointments. Massive basilica churches started appearing during the time of the newly converted emperor Constantine (†337); in a city like Rome these ancient basilicas have been adorned and expanded in the seventeen hundred years since Constantine's time. Yet one of the major conflicts that Christians experienced concerned the place of icons, those glorious mosaics that are part of Eastern devotion. In Eastern Christianity there were conflicts over the use of icons in the eighth and ninth centuries, with opponents urging that icons should not even exist. Some classical music, too, was written for magnificent presentation in large churches; many would argue that the beauty and glory of the music detracts, ironically, from the meaning of the worship. "They come for the music, not for God"—this could be said of many eras in Christian life.

The misuse of glory revolves around employing beauty for its own sake and not as something that points beyond itself, to God. By the same token, then, using glory to call people's attention to God seems to make great spiritual sense. Drawing the line between misuse and proper use might, however, be difficult. It has become standard today, in some lines of thinking, for "experts" to say that hearing congregations applaud shows that worship has been abused. "You are applauding the talent of the musicians or the preacher; you are not focused on God as you should be." But what if beauty, of its nature, draws one to God? What if some cultures use applause to signal an excess of devotion, not an absence of it? Does the ecstatic always mean quiet kneeling? Might it not also show itself in shouts and clapping?

Transfiguration

Mark's Gospel is so matter of fact we are almost stunned when we come upon the scene that we have come to call the transfiguration (Mark 9:2ff.). Throughout Mark's Gospel we see Jesus doing powerful deeds of the Kingdom, but many of these are pitched in a special way against the forces of darkness (e.g., 5:1ff.). Mark begins to narrate how much opposition developed against Jesus early in his Gospel (3:6), so Jesus seems to be always working under pressure. Mark goes out of his way to emphasize Jesus as the servant who suffers, who gives of himself in humility, who comes "not...to be served but to serve and to give his life as a ransom for many" (10:45). In fact, his followers almost always completely miss this point about Jesus. They are jockeying for prestige and influence while Jesus keeps his eyes on the place of his humiliation and suffering. Jesus emphasizes that being Messiah is to be a servant (10:45), to be lowly and to give his life. Jesus, throughout the early chapters of Mark, even tries to hide who he is.

This pressure comes to a boil in the eighth chapter of Mark, when Jesus asks his disciples who they think he is. Peter famously proclaims, "You are the Messiah," after which Jesus sternly warns his disciples not to tell anyone about him. But right at this moment Jesus, now proclaimed the Messiah, or the Christ, starts to predict what will happen to him: "The Son of Man must suffer greatly and be rejected by the elders, the chief priests, and the scribes, and be killed, and rise after three days" (Mark 8:27–32). The drama of Jesus's ministry, having come to one climactic point (being named Messiah), now proceeds onto an even more dramatic point (Jesus's death and resurrection).

This is when Mark presents the story of the transfiguration, a story all the more remarkable given the relentless way Mark has portrayed Jesus's lowliness and suffering. Mark's story happens shortly after Jesus's first prediction of his death and resurrection. It is Mark's way of attributing explicitly divine qualities to Jesus even as he presents Jesus as the servant destined to suffer. In other words, in a persistently dark and sober account of Jesus, here is the one point when the curtains are pulled back and Jesus shows the hallmarks of glory. Themes of light were associated with the idea of glory since the Book of Exodus, notably the fire and cloud that accompanied the Jewish people and Moses's encounters with God on the mountain and in the meeting tent (Exod 40:34). These stories themselves appear to be stamped with influences of Jewish worship in the temple, particularly the clouds of incense that accompanied Jewish worship (1 Kgs 8:12; Isa 1:2–4).

Something like worship happens on this mountain where Jesus radiates forth another view of who he is. The words in Mark basically say Jesus "changed his form." Was the form of brilliant light always around Jesus but people could not see it clearly? Mark certainly teaches us that this form of glory was part of the reality of Jesus, that is to say, part of the reality of Jesus being the Messiah destined to suffer and rise. Jesus anticipates the fullness that would show in his rising from the dead; the followers of Jesus share in that anticipation. Glory is already a force in our present lives as we look ahead into a future of the fullness of life.

In Mark's account, Jesus brings his "inner circle" of disciples (Peter, James, and John who were initially called by him in Galilee) up a "high mountain," and "he was transfigured before them, and his clothes became dazzling white" (Mark 9:2–3). Moses and Elijah now join Jesus in conversation; two key figures of Jewish faith, both of whom had mysterious deaths: when Moses dies, no one knows where he is buried (Deut 34:6); when Elijah's mission ends, he is taken up in a chariot (2 Kgs 2:11). What, then, would happen with Jesus's death? Interestingly in Luke's version of this story, the three are explicitly talking about the journey (the Greek text literally says *exodus*) Jesus would accomplish (Luke 9:31) in Jerusalem, a clear reference to Jesus's death and resurrection.

The inner circle seemingly does not know what to do when confronted with this different form that Jesus showed when he went to the top of the mountain. Peter suggests making three tents, one for each of the figures in conversation. Mark comments, "He hardly knew what to say, they were so terrified" (Mark 9:6). Peter represents all of us on the edge of the mysterious: we want to keep things safe in our tents, but we really do not know what we are dealing with. For it is exactly at this moment, when Peter suggests the tents, that a cloud comes upon all of them; from that cloud comes the voice from heaven that makes the point of the whole scene clear: "This my beloved Son. Listen to him" (9:7). The glory of Jesus is to articulate the vision and the way of the Father. We must listen to, pay close attention to, Jesus's way of life and his journey.

Mark resolves the tension between light and darkness, excitement and fear, in the simplest way. "Suddenly, looking around, they no longer saw anyone but Jesus alone with them" (9:8). In the end it was just as it was in the beginning, only Jesus with his disciples. The relationship Jesus has with his disciples, including both the brilliant and the dark moments, is a relationship Jesus has with all who follow him. A disciple's life will, at times, seem glorious but, at other moments, feel like emptiness. However it might look and feel, Jesus never refuses his presence.

The glory of Jesus reveals the pattern of the experiences that we believers have. We carry our ultimate destiny with us, making it either the path along which we walk or else, for the unfortunate, the vision against which we fight. For those who follow the path of Jesus, our *exodus*, our passage to freedom and fullness, is already underway for us. A future of fullness is already upon us. For most followers of Jesus, that fullness breaks at times into the present moments of our lives, although rarely as stunningly as it did for Jesus. As the disciples learned, so we learn: Christ's glory abides with him whether that is visible to us or not.

John, in his Gospel, does not have the story of the transfiguration but, in a way, he doesn't need it. John has plenty of glory, however. In one place in that Gospel, Jesus says,

> I glorified you on earth by accomplishing the work that you gave me to do. Now glorify me, Father, with you, with the glory that I had with you before the world began. (John 17:4–5)

Earlier in that same Gospel, Jesus says, "Father, glorify your name." Then a voice came from heaven, "I have glorified it and will glorify it again" (12:28). In fact, the glory of Jesus is his being "lifted up" as a sign of God's love for the world, a glory that, in John's Gospel, dovetails with the resurrection of Jesus.

A spirituality of the Kingdom sees glory shot through all existence but hardly in the sense of a royal coronation or some Hollywood concept of fame. The glory of the Kingdom stems from what God accomplishes in and through those who give themselves in love to others. This spiritual vision does not concentrate on the dark and empty moments any more than it seeks for the consolation of sparkling moments. Rather, all moments, however they seem, rush forward to God's vision of a Kingdom where love and life have reached their fullness. The best expressions of glorious art in Christian life simply bring this longed-for vision to greater concentration.

A spirituality for the Kingdom means living with the voice of Christ as our guide: "Listen to him" (Mark 9:7). He leads us on our journeys, whether up mountains or down valleys, whether filled with light or overshadowed with clouds, whether bearing moments of acceptance or those of rejection. As he leads us, we anticipate resurrection because we share in the Spirit of the risen Christ. As he leads us, resurrection becomes more actual in our lives and, therefore, in the world.

Reflection: The Glory of Heaven

What will heaven's glory be like? Will it be the city coming down out of the sky with streets paved with gold, with jewels on all the walls that surround the city, as the

*Book of Revelation puts it (Rev 21:2)? Will there be prover-
bial gates of pearl?*

*The story of the transfiguration gives us a solid hint,
I think. For Jesus's face becomes radiant, as if what was
inside Jesus could finally be revealed by the face gazing
upon us. Hollywood has quite a time trying to depict spiritual and heavenly radiance; the directors of movies and
video have lots of ways to project light onto faces to make
them radiant. A little bit of makeup also serves the purpose.*

*But what about the radiance we see in each other's
faces from time to time? A mother gazes around at the
faces of her family after a special meal has been shared.
An old man, in a hospital bed, looks up at one who has
come to visit. A father walks his daughter down the aisle.
The twenty-two-year-old walks on the stage to receive her
diploma. An office team sings a Christmas carol at the
end of a party and some eyes glisten with tears. A young
woman rises out of the baptismal font on Easter. Best
friends finally can see each other after spending their first
semester at different schools, their smiles unstoppable.
The faces of children we see in procession to receive holy
communion linger for days in our memories.*

*Each of us has hundreds of memories of radiant
faces we have seen. But why do they radiate? It's not just
the lighting or the occasion; those are factors that bring
out something deeper. A loving bond of beloved and lover
makes these faces shine. Love and being loved makes us
beam; the radiance is our faces' way of saying how much
we are present for each other in love.*

*This helps, a little, for our vision of heaven. We won't
be thinking about the clouds, or the harps, or the pearly
gates. Heaven will be the realization of the depth of love
that has bound humankind together. The radiance of*

93

heaven will be the possibility of our fully being able to express how bound we are to others, how close we have dared to come, and how much more we wanted to give of ourselves for those we've loved.

Our faces will finally be able to reveal the full extent of our hearts' desires. All who have glimpsed of this vision and tried to live it in their own way will amplify the transparent joy we have found in one another because of the radiance of God's face, of God's unbounded love, beaming upon us and shining through us. We will all be Moses and Elijah, Mary and John the Baptist; we will all be transfixed in each other's presence, astounded at what God's love has created, redeemed, and graced. There may be words, but they won't be necessary. We will finally be able to see, and show, divine brilliance, now shared and lived to the full.

> *...and we saw his glory,*
> *the glory as of the Father's only Son,*
> *full of grace and truth. (John 1:14)*

~ • ~

For Discussion and Reflection

Read this passage slowly.

Luke 9:28–36

About eight days after he said this, he took Peter, John, and James and went up the mountain to pray. While he was praying his face changed in appearance and his clothing became dazzling white. And behold, two men were conversing with him, Moses and Elijah, who appeared in glory and spoke of his exodus that he was going to accomplish in Jerusalem. Peter and his companions had been overcome by sleep, but becoming fully awake, they saw his glory and the two men standing with him. As they were about to part from him, Peter said to Jesus, "Master, it is good that we are here; let us make three tents, one for you, one for Moses, and one for Elijah." But he did not know what he was saying. While he was still speaking, a cloud came and cast a shadow over them, and they became frightened when they entered the cloud. Then from the cloud came a voice that said, "This is my chosen Son; listen to him." After the voice had spoken, Jesus was found alone. They fell silent and did not at that time tell anyone what they had seen.

1. Would you have liked to have been on the mountain with Peter, John, and James? Explain your answer, including how this scene makes you feel.
2. In what way does this scene help you know what Jesus thought of himself as "Messiah"?
3. Why do you think the cloud overshadows the disciples and God speaks from the cloud to them? What do you think is happening at this point?

Slowly pray the Lord's Prayer and conclude by asking God's blessing on you and yours.

Chapter 7

BRINGING THE KINGDOM TO BIRTH

IF THE LIFE OF JESUS was fixed on the Kingdom of God, both as a way of life and as a future for humankind; if his wonder-filled deeds and his words all harkened to a new human reality of life filled with unbounded love; if he became aware of profound conflicts with religious leaders at his time: how, then, did he see his death?

Most people have unremarkable deaths inasmuch as they die alone or with a few people in a hospital or nursing home. A few people have deaths that can be framed by their lives, so notable were their careers. Certainly, national leaders and famous people have large funerals, sometimes lasting for days, with many people to comment on their legacy. These days many are tempted to spin their own lives in certain directions as they make videos of themselves to be played at wakes or even funerals. Some people during human or medical crises may have time to reflect on their lives; hospice has come as one clear, modern blessing to those who are terminally ill, allowing both the ill and their caregivers time to reflect and share. Many are robbed of this opportunity because death comes out of nowhere, sudden and final.

Here was Jesus, totally dedicated to inaugurating

the Kingdom of God and certainly aware of a relationship with his Father that was intimate and unique, beginning his ministry right in the wake of the arrest of John the Baptist. Here was Jesus healing people in front of leaders who attacked him, questioned his motives, and even plotted against him. Here was Jesus raising people from the dead as he faced his own probable death.

But out of this tension between Jesus's vision and the opposition he received, the Kingdom would come to birth.

Conflict

At some point it must have become clear to Jesus that, however he thought about his ministry, conflict and rejection would be part of accomplishing his work. The central insight would have to revolve precisely around "accomplishing his work": How does defeat lead to accomplishing a mission? How does humiliating failure translate into success? Was his agony in the garden the night before his death (Luke 22:44) a taste not only of the bitterness of human pain now pressing upon him but, even more, the bitterness of a mission that seemed doomed?

Jesus must have had moments of great clarity about this. What gave him the ability to predict his own rejection? What allows him to stare Peter down when Peter refuses to acknowledge the destiny Jesus foresaw, when he calls Peter a "Satan"—that is, one who tests and temps him (Mark 8:33)? Clearly it was the vision of his Father who grounded his life, experience, and mission. People cannot live for causes that might lead to their death without a central vision. The twentieth century gave us

Mahatma Gandhi, Martin Luther King Jr., and Mother Teresa as contemporary examples of this.

Jesus also has a vision of the Kingdom of God, that new state of existence that his Father willed; when he calls himself "Son of Man," he acknowledges, in effect, his central role in the Kingdom's revelation. He also has little fear. When warned that Herod was after him, Jesus asks his hearers to tell "that fox" that he would be preaching for two more days before moving on (Luke 13:32). Such sense of purpose would allow him to be silent in front of the political leader, Pontius Pilate, who would tolerate his murder (Mark 15:5).

There is a line in Luke's Gospel that gives us a big clue to Jesus's thinking. "Yet I must continue on my way today, tomorrow, and the following day, for it is impossible that a prophet should die outside of Jerusalem," says Jesus (Luke 13:33). Luke's Gospel has already shown how Jesus was determined to go to Jerusalem as an inherent part of the divine project he was called to accomplish: "When the days for his being taken up were fulfilled, he resolutely determined to journey to Jerusalem" (9:51). In other words, Jesus saw serving the Kingdom as part of his destiny, part of what a prophet must be ready for, even if that destiny involved being rejected and assassinated.

Perhaps it seems almost contradictory to think that the proclamation of the Kingdom of God would involve the death of the Kingdom's Messiah, the beloved One chosen to inaugurate it. Yet this was the conclusion of the followers of Jesus as they absorbed the tragedy of his death and experienced his resurrection appearances. When Jesus is walking with the two disciples toward Emmaus on Easter morning, he says to them, it seems with a bit of frustration, "Was it not necessary that the

Messiah should suffer these things and enter into his glory?" (Luke 24:26). There was something inevitable about the death of Jesus, given the built-in conflict that was part of the birth of the Kingdom of God.

We can certainly try to imagine an alternative universe in which Jesus, vastly improving on Jonah's very effective preaching, might have convinced people to accept his message and become part of the Kingdom without any resistance or conflict. But that wasn't the world Jesus lived in. When we think about our own resistance to the Kingdom, shown through our own coldness and sinfulness, we realize just how fanciful such an alternative imagined world has to be. Conflict always stood ready.

Death

People have had different ways of reflecting on this outcome of murder at the end of Jesus's preaching and ministry. Christians have long thought that Christ's death was the result of human sin, which merited death; Jesus, though sinless, dies because of our sins and so frees us from sin's consequences and from death. Jesus's death could also be seen as the result of his humanity; if he hadn't died by crucifixion, he might well have died some other, perhaps less violent, way. It would have been part of God's redemption by taking on the fullness of our lives in Jesus.

But Jesus's death might be better viewed as the deliberate way he went about showing us the future that God was opening up for us. In other words, Jesus overcomes sin by undergoing death in order to reveal the resurrection as an essential dimension of the Kingdom. Going to Jerusalem as a martyr, one who bears witness to God's truth, Jesus affirms that truth in his words and deeds. When those very words and deeds engender rejection and scorn, Jesus faces these as expressions of the very sin that must be conquered and vanquished in humankind. Resurrection, as the definitive sign of mercy and reconciliation, brings about a new state of existence in which people, reconciled to God, begin to experience the Kingdom.

In this way, Jesus indeed dies because of our sin but not fundamentally because of some notion of justice that God must adhere to, as if Jesus's God did not know about mercy! Jesus dies as the revelation of God's reconciliation with humankind, opening a future that humans foreclosed for themselves. Along with justice, people also associate the idea of sacrifice with Jesus's death. But sacrifice does not need to be understood as a vicious killing that God's justice demanded. Rather, sacrifice can be understood as part of an entire process of reconciliation. Jewish people brought sacrifices (animal or grain) to the temple so that they might experience peace and unity with God through the sacred meal that followed. What sacrifice accomplished in Jewish worship, Jesus brings about by his death and resurrection: reconciliation and union with God. God initiates the great work of mercy through the gift of Jesus's death and resurrection.

Jesus, inaugurating the Kingdom, sees that his own death will open for humankind a vision of life that humankind needs to understand itself. For once Jesus is raised, we can no longer think of ourselves only as more highly evolved animal, but animal nonetheless; or only as relatively unimportant creatures in a mindless universe; or only as victims of our own shame and hatred. Resurrection shows us the status humankind has always had before God, we who are called to enduring relationship with the divine in such a way that dignity, hope, and life become part of the way we can understand ourselves.

At the event we call the Last Supper, Jesus gives some indication of how he sees his upcoming death. During the ceremonial drinking of the cups of wine, Jesus says, "Amen, I say to you, I shall not drink again the fruit of the vine until the day when I drink it new in the kingdom of God" (Mark 14:25). Obviously, Jesus is looking ahead to his passion but also looking through his passion to something yet beyond. The Kingdom will be the reality more fully available for humankind after Jesus dies and rises. This is why our continued sharing in the sacred meal of Jesus, shown at the Last Supper, means that we are part of the "new and eternal covenant" that Jesus established, making valid and real all God's covenants with humankind (Mark 14:24). Jesus gives us the reconciling meal that accompanies our ability to draw close to God—because God has drawn close to us in mercy. This covenant gives us the possibility of sharing in the future Jesus revealed in his death and resurrection; every time the Church celebrates the Eucharist it embodies in sacrament God's destiny for humankind.

This perspective, then, allows us to look at all the events at the Last Supper as an anticipation of the eschatological realities for which Jesus lived and died. The shared bread is, indeed, a participation in Jesus's body that is being handed over; the cup is a sharing in the blood of the "new and eternal" covenant that Jesus secures in his dying and rising. But the broken body and the spent blood of Jesus not only look backward to those terrible moments of abandonment and agony; they look forward to the heavenly banquet in which the sweep of humankind will be united and sustained through the work of Jesus the Messiah. As Paul puts it when writing to the Corinthians: "For as often as you eat this bread and drink the cup, you proclaim the death of the Lord until he comes" (1 Cor 11:26). The coming of the Lord is the explicit message of every Eucharist that we celebrate. As his final gesture with his disciples, then, in spite of all their missteps in understanding him, Jesus gives them a sharing in the messianic event that will bring the Kingdom more fully into reality. They share in the end-times because they share in Jesus's breaking the limits of death, of time, in his sacrificial act.

The act is sacrificial in two senses. First, Jesus has to push himself to fulfill the destiny given him, the destiny he has accepted. In the Garden of Gethsemane, before his arrest, we find him pleading to his Father: "Abba, Father, all things are possible to you. Take this cup away from me, but not what I will but what you will" (Mark 14:36). Having identified with humanity, Jesus now experiences humanity in terms of sheer horror and repulsion; he also experiences humanity in terms of the irrational violence humans are capable of conjuring.

Second, Jesus becomes a sacrifice himself. As Paul summarizes it, it is Jesus "whom God set forth as an expiation, through faith, by his blood, to prove his righteousness because of the forgiveness of sins previously committed" (Rom 3:25). On this reading Jesus is not a sacrifice we offer but a sacrifice that God places before us, one that proves God's commitment to "make things right" through his mercy, one in which we can partake. We also find in the First Letter of John the following: "In this is love: not that we have loved God, but that he loved us and sent his Son as expiation for our sins" (1 John 4:10). So God takes the initiative for this very overcoming of sin. Just as reconciliation and peace were accomplished in some way through the offerings the Jewish people made to God, allowing for propitiation (= unity), so God makes the offering of Jesus, his Son, an unending place of propitiation and unity for humankind. Jesus doesn't merely "pay the price" for our sins as it is put frequently; he is God's gift to humankind and to creation to show reconciliation through the coming of the Kingdom.

One of the clearest signs of the reconciling action of the crucifixion occurs in Luke's Gospel, with an incident that only he presents. On either side of Jesus hang two criminals. In all likelihood, these men were involved in criminal conspiracy against the occupation of Rome. We flatter them when we call them thieves. One of these criminals joins in the scorn many directed at Jesus, just the kind of humiliation and dehumanization that the Romans designed crucifixion to accomplish. The other criminal, however, remarks on how much they, as criminals, deserve capital punishment, but not Jesus. He then looks over to Jesus and requests, "Jesus, remember me when you come into your kingdom." To which Jesus replies, "Amen, I say to you, today you will be with me in Paradise" (Luke 23:42–43).

Jesus clearly envisions a new domain that he was opening up through his martyr's death. Luke reinforces this memorable act of mercy on the part of Jesus by showing him crying out on the cross, "Father, forgive them, they know not what they do" (Luke 23:34). This means that mercy and forgiveness now define the realm that Jesus accomplishes in his death. Mercy and pardon open people up to a new future because they do not have to keep looking back in shame or regret. Forgiveness concerns the future far more than the past by breaking down alienation and making reconciliation happen.

The Gospels of Matthew and Mark have Jesus crying out a phrase that comes close to scandalizing believers:

"My God, my God, why have you forsaken me?" (Mark 15:34; Matt 27:46). We realize these words as the start of a psalm that ultimately proclaims the vindication of those in distress through the power of God, Psalm 22. Nevertheless, we cannot miss the utter tension behind these words that Jesus experiences: the tension between our ultimate experience of time (death, when time is no more) and a vision suffused with a boundless horizon. To be forsaken echoes every dying person's deepest fear; to cry that out on the cross is to cry before the world exactly what the stakes are in terms of Jesus accomplishing his mission. Through abandonment and death, done as a sign of God's mercy and reconciliation, Jesus opens for humankind a yet deeper revelation of the Kingdom.

In Luke's Gospel we find a different kind of abandonment. Jesus abandons himself into the hands of his loving Father. The one proclaimed "beloved Son" at his baptism and in the transfiguration now claims that sonship through an act of total trust. Luke portrays the drama of the moment with darkness and storms; then he writes, "Jesus cried out in a loud voice, 'Father, into your hands I commend my spirit'; and when he had said this he breathed his last" (Luke 23:46). By placing himself in the hands of his Father, and by making it possible for all to place themselves in God's hands as well, Jesus shows the boundless future available to all who are part of the Kingdom because of their primal trust in the Father. In case we resist the idea of the crucifixion being the passageway to the future, Matthew recounts a strange scene unique to his Gospel:

> The earth quaked, rocks were split, tombs were
> opened, and the bodies of many saints who had
> fallen asleep were raised. And coming forth from

their tombs after his resurrection, they entered the holy city and appeared to many. (Matt 27:51–53)

The martyr's death that Jesus accepted accomplishes its purpose of showing the sweeping potential for humankind and for all creation. The crucifixion was even more an event of new life than mainly an event of tragic death.

Resurrection

John's language about Jesus's death underlines something implicit in the other accounts. After Jesus says, "It is finished," he bows his head and he "handed over the spirit," as the original Greek language reads it (see John 19:30). The first phrase could easily be translated as "it is accomplished" or even "it is brought to completion." This confirms the notion that Jesus's death was part of the larger message of proclaiming and bringing the Kingdom of God.

The second phrase can also be translated as "he passed on his spirit." The death of Jesus brings us into a new world in which the Kingdom begins to be revealed as a world in which God's Spirit is freely poured upon humankind so that the vision of Jesus—a world renewed by hope and freed from the distortions that limit it— would continue to be realized. Such a world, in some ways a twilight world where things are both obscure and hauntingly clear at the same time, can be glimpsed in the scattered events that the Bible gives us about Jesus's resurrection and the disciples' first experience of him in his risen life. But these very scattered images seem perfectly appropriate for a world on the cusp of transformation, sensing something new that has happened and trying to capture that newness.

On Easter morning, creation awakes and, groggy, begins to realize that today has begun to merge with tomorrow, that the present has become a passageway into an unlimited future.

Mark's Gospel ends very abruptly; a longer ending was composed for this Gospel, but it seems to be a compilation of the various accounts of Easter we find in other places in the New Testament. But Mark's shorter ending communicates well what it means to be in tension, to be suspended between what we have experienced and what we are barely able to anticipate. In Mark's account, like the other Gospel accounts, the women who have followed Jesus and have noted where Jesus was buried are now hastening to his tomb to anoint his body with oils and fragrances. This idea was obviously spontaneous and unplanned because they had not thought of the problem of removing the stone from the tomb. But when they arrive, these women see that removing the stone was not the issue; rather, they had to confront the reality that Jesus has been raised from the dead. They had to begin figuring what this meant for Jesus, but, even more, what it meant for them and, potentially, for all humankind.

As Mark puts it:

When they looked up, they saw that the stone had been rolled back; it was very large. On entering the tomb they saw a young man sitting on the right side, clothed in a white robe, and they were utterly amazed. He said to them, "Do not be amazed! You seek Jesus of Nazareth, the crucified. He has been raised; he is not here. Behold, the place where they laid him. But go

and tell his disciples and Peter, 'He is going
before you to Galilee; there you will see him, as
he told you.'" Then they went out and fled from
the tomb, seized with trembling and bewilder-
ment. They said nothing to anyone, for they
were afraid. (Mark 16:4–8)

This account is hardly an auspicious start to Easter, but
it captures the twilight quality of Easter experiences,
the doubts and the needed clarifications, the fear and
the intimations. It shows one of our possible attitudes
to the vision of the future: running away in fear, saying
nothing, shutting down. Can it be that this is the usual
state of our human consciousness? Recall Plato's famous
image: that humans mostly live in a "cave"; we think the
limitations of the cave, the dimness of light, is all there
is. How do we open our hearts to the possibilities that
God has for us, the possibilities of the Kingdom?

Fortunately, the other accounts of Easter do not end
in fearful silence. In Matthew's Gospel, as the women
are running away, they actually meet the risen Christ.
"And behold, Jesus met them on their way and greeted
them. They approached, embraced his feet, and did him
homage. Then Jesus said to them, 'Do not be afraid. Go
tell my brothers to go to Galilee, and there they will see
me'" (Matt 28:9–10). Here the women arc commissioned
both by the messenger in the tomb and by Jesus himself
to bring a message of hope to the disciples. The women
encounter Jesus, seek to draw near to him, but then hear
Jesus tell them to bring news to others.

John's Gospel give us fuller pictures of what encounter with the risen Jesus is like. On his telling, Mary
Magdalene comes to the tomb and sees the stone moved
away. She immediately runs back to the disciples, two

of whom then run to the tomb and look in. One disciple, Peter, takes careful note of the burial robes neatly folded in the tomb; the other disciple with Peter then enters and comes to believe when he sees the burial robes. "For they did not yet understand the scripture that he had to rise from the dead," John tells us (John 20:9). Although the disciples return home, Mary Magdalene stays at the tomb weeping.

She mistakes the risen Christ for a gardener (how frequently Jesus is misidentified in the Easter stories!) and questions him about Jesus's missing body. But when Jesus calls her name, Mary, "she turned and said to him in Hebrew, 'Rabouni,' which means Teacher." Mary then falls to the ground, approaching Jesus and holding on to him. But Jesus bids her not to hold on to him but rather to tell his disciples that "I am going to my Father and your Father, to my God and your God" (John 20:16–17). Mary can now drop the fearful silence that characterized the first reaction to the risen Christ. Indeed, she runs to the disciples with a very clear message, the first proclamation of Easter from human lips: "I have seen the Lord," she says (20:18).

When Jesus encounters his disciples, the greater scope of the project of the Kingdom becomes clearer. Keeping the theme of fearful silence, the disciples are behind locked doors; that evening of his resurrection, Jesus comes and stands before them because locks are no barrier to the message of Easter. Jesus's first words describe the aspect of God toward these men and toward the world: "Peace be with you." The risen Christ first of all brings the announcement of reconciliation, to people fearful and hiding, to people who ran in fear, indeed, to people who have no dream of a future. Reconciliation now opens up something new to human experience.

Jesus next shows them his hands and feet. The future that God brings about does not deny the scars of human experience. Indeed, those scars are a way to show how human brokenness has been transcended, how the heaven we long for does not erase the limitations of earth. The scars clearly help to identify Jesus as the one who was crucified; they also verify that Jesus is not a ghost or hologram; this is the same One who loved them. The joy the disciples experience echoes all the way back to the abundance of wine at the wedding feast of Cana. Not only is a town dancing; creation itself has begun to dance in the body of the risen Christ.

Next Jesus evokes the Holy Spirit, the "spirit" that he passed on to humankind at his death. "As the Father has sent me, so I send you," he says (John 20:21). With this powerful line Jesus creates new momentum in his followers and in all humankind. How did the Father send Jesus? To be an effective sign of joy and hope, to include people otherwise excluded because of physical limitations or social constraints, to give sight to people who never thought they could see, to proclaim that one's relationship with God endured through life and death into new life, to bend down and wash the feet of people who felt unworthy to be washed. Jesus imparts his vision of looking beyond himself toward a life filled with hope and joy to these men staring in amazement at his risen body.

This vision is part of what Jesus means when he bids them to "receive the holy Spirit" (John 20:22). What spirit would they receive but the very one that accompanied Jesus through all his ministry, the Spirit that came down at his baptism, the Spirit that Jesus described as a spring of water that would surge endlessly, the Spirit that was with him through death and resurrection? As the Father has empowered his Son through the Holy Spirit, so Jesus now empowers his followers who have life, energy, vision, and hope because Jesus has been raised and now shares his resurrection with those who open their hearts to him.

The encounter with the risen Christ, filled with God's eternal Spirit, now is replicated as Jesus's followers encounter each other, humankind, and humankind's boundless future.

As this happens, the potentialities embedded in creation begin to be revealed, drawn forth by the revelation of God's unbounded mercy and love. Matter and energy, electrons and protons, eons of subtle change, the formation of stars and planets, the evolution of life and human being: all receives direction in the risen body of Christ.

Meditation: Life as Encounter

When I look back at my life, now more than seven decades, I certainly remember distinct events. Like many, however, the events designed precisely to be memorable seem the haziest, like my ordination to be a priest. Likewise, what do I remember of receiving confirmation? It's easier to remember the big events in the lives of others than to recall my own.

But, far more than events, I remember encounters, times when friends and loved ones seemed powerfully close. With memories of these people, in the various situations in which I recall them, it's as if they become present once again, not for any other purpose than to be present, to rejoice in the glow of "mere" existence. These encounters, spread over a lifetime, seem to make up my soul, my inner life. These encounters appear, more and more, like the substance of human experience itself. Such experiences seem to me to be what life is all about.

Jesus brings the Kingdom to birth by encountering us in his risen glory, a glory that emerged from the very conflicts and oppositions of his life but, even more, from the fixedness of the vision he had of doing the will of his Father, that is, of bringing the Kingdom about. He rises from the dead to become part of the encounters that make up our human experience. When he encounters us, when he lets us encounter him, the glory of his resurrection, the splendor of the Kingdom, begins to glow more powerfully. When he encounters us, he gives us his Spirit.

~ • ~

For Reflection and Discussion

Read the following passage slowly.

John 2:13–33

Since the Passover of the Jews was near, Jesus went up to Jerusalem. He found in the temple area those who sold oxen, sheep, and doves, as well as the money-changers seated there. He made a whip out of cords and drove them all out of the temple area, with the sheep and oxen, and spilled the coins of the money-changers and overturned their tables, and to those who sold doves he said, "Take these out of here, and stop making my Father's house a marketplace." His disciples recalled the words of Scripture, "Zeal for your house will consume me." At this the Jews answered and said to him, "What sign can you show us for doing this?" Jesus answered and said to them, "Destroy this temple and in three days I will raise it up." The Jews said, "This temple has been under construction for forty-six years, and you will raise it up in three days?" But he was speaking about the temple of his body. Therefore, when he was raised from the dead, his disciples remembered that he had said this, and they came to believe the Scripture and the word Jesus had spoken.

1. How do you understand the conflict that this passage from John presents to us?
2. In what ways do you think of Jesus as a temple? What does this image of Jesus as a temple mean to you?
3. How does this passage help you understand the salvation that Jesus was bringing to the world?

Slowly pray the Lord's Prayer and conclude by asking God's blessing on you and yours.

Chapter 8

SPIRIT: BRINGING CREATION TO THE KINGDOM

JOACHIM OF FIORE (†1202) enjoyed widespread fame in his time. Living right after St. Dominic and St. Francis, founders, respectively, of the Dominicans and the Franciscans, Joachim thought a new era was dawning for the Church. He called it the "third reign"—the reign of the Holy Spirit. In his scriptural reading and meditations, Joachim saw the time of the Old Testament as the time of the Father; he conceived the first thousand years of Christian life as the time of the Son. But now there would begin a time of the Holy Spirit when humankind would enter a new era, institutions would be unnecessary, and the Spirit would reign in the world.

Joachim's writings and teaching did not come to much prominence in the Church, which, perhaps, is not surprising given the way his teaching could lead to strange interpretations and behaviors. What should shock us is that he could look upon the Church of his times, a Church in which he had a very active and spiritual role, and not see the Spirit already at work in the first millennium of Christian life. The outpouring of the Holy Spirit, harbinger of the new world that God is already bringing about, was the legacy Christ gave to his people. As the Spirit worked in Christ's life producing, with the Son, signs of a new world breaking upon human history, so Christ continues his work in that same Spirit that he sends freely upon us. "[God] does not ration his gift of the Spirit" (John 3:34).

Uniting

Luke gives us a glimpse of what the Spirit might mean to the Kingdom as he begins the Book of Acts. In the second chapter, he narrates an event that Christians call Pentecost. This is not long after Jesus "departs" from the disciples; that is, his Easter presence in one form now becomes a presence in diverse forms. Christian life is an ever-expanding recognition of the diversity of forms of divine presence in our lives.

Although depicted on a much larger scale, the same Easter pattern of initial fear and hesitation continues: the disciples are staying enclosed, among themselves. We feel they have the same fear that the women showed at first that early Easter morning. Although the disciples had formed a distinct community, joined in prayer, they did not know what to do. Suddenly, however, a strong, driving wind begins to fill the house where they are enclosed; tongues like fire appear over them. Their silence now breaks apart not from their own decision but from the power of the Spirit within them. Now they have found their voice; now they can speak.

They are even surprised by their own speech because they speak in all kinds of languages, "as the Spirit enabled them to proclaim" (Acts 2:4). Luke uses this image to

114

portray, in a symbolic way, one of the most important advances in human experience—a consequence of the resurrection of Jesus Christ. Believers in Jesus, through the Spirit, begin to form communities that crossed national and language boundaries. Although Jewish believers from all over the Mediterranean region had assembled in Jerusalem for the Feast of Pentecost, each of these people, representing the nations of the world, can now hear the message of God's love in her or his own language.

It takes but a moment to think about the Tower of Babel in the Book of Genesis, how the overweening ambition of humans to build a temple that reached into heaven itself (undoubtedly a reference to various non-Jewish forms of worship) resulted in human division, language against language, tribe against tribe, nation against nation (Gen 11:1ff.). The section begins with an ideal image: "The whole world had the same language and the same words" (Gen 11:1), but it ends with the stark reality of those human divisions that have caused so much hatred, violence, and death: "The LORD confused the speech of all the world" (Gen 11:9).

How much human destruction can we trace back to human divisions? The idea, surely, isn't that if we all spoke one language everything would be great. Rather, the idea is that our different languages reveal deeper divisions within us, divisions that lead some to think they are stronger, some to consider themselves as superior, some to judge others, some to construe "the other" as evil and liable to destruction. In the modern world, where communications can lead different ethnic groups to form a larger grouping, these larger groups then enter into conflict, all looking for some advantage over another. Totalitarian movements, whether from the right or the left, scarred the whole of the twentieth century with destruction made all that much more wretched because technology had enhanced the capacity of humans to destroy each other. The trenches of World War I link with the atomic bombs that ended World War II.

What we see happening at the Pentecost event stands as an alternative to the whole thrust of separating, dividing, and vanquishing that has composed most of human history. Luke's passage in Acts 2 almost goes out of its way listing the various peoples from all around who can now grasp, and respond, to a new message of salvation. "We are Parthians, Medes, and Elamites...yet we hear them speaking in our own tongues of the mighty acts of God" (Acts 2:9–11). A new message, with a new vision of humankind, was generated in the experience of Pentecost, one with essential importance for human possibilities. For Pentecost represents the possibility of an international union of people bound by love, all of them living for the values that Jesus demonstrated in his life, death, and resurrection.

We see two immediate effects of this new way of life. First, we see the earliest disciples doing in their own lives what Jesus did, particularly in their outreach to the poor, the handicapped, the excluded. This outreach also meant preaching the risen Christ to groups who were either despised in Jewish reckoning or completely alien; for example, Ethiopians (Acts 8:26ff.), Gentiles (Acts 11:1ff.), and Samaritans (8:5, 9). One of the key developments in the Book of Acts is Paul's decision to reach out to Macedonia and bring the Christian message into what today we call Europe (Acts 16:9ff.). Within thirty years of Jesus's departure from the disciples, his followers had communities in many different countries and cultures;

they were also writing in Greek, the international language of that time.

Second, as a result of this outreach, Christian-formed communities were novel in the ancient world: people of very different social statuses, income levels, and races now gathered in fellowship, all washed in the same sacrament of baptism, and all gathered to receive the same Eucharist. We can look at the various people to whom Paul sends greetings at the end of his letters, noting the blend of different names and the different positions they held with reference to their society.

The sending of the Holy Spirit brought about a growing community of people linked by an experience of divine love and the celebration of simple but powerful rituals. Love was at the heart of these communities: the capacity to live selflessly for others even at great cost to oneself. People would be able to recognize Christians by the love they showed (John 13:35). The love a Christian showed would be marked by gentleness and humility, a reverence for each person, and a reverence for creation itself.

Striving for a new world in which love reigned and each person was cherished constituted the central commitment for people who worshiped in the name of the One who gave his life that tomorrow might dawn on people today. "Thy kingdom come" echoed on their lips. This prayer not only beckoned a future world; it described the world they believed they were already living in because they had experienced the Holy Spirit through their mutual love, celebrated sacraments that brought them into unity with the risen Christ, strove for an integrity of life that exceeded the expectations of their ancient cultures, and lived as if death were no longer the ultimate barrier in life.

Living

St. Paul gives us a remarkable line in the Letter to the Romans: "...and hope does not disappoint, because the love of God has been poured out into our hearts through the holy Spirit that has been given to us" (Rom 5:5). This could be one of the best ways to speak about conversion, that change of mentality that allows us to see the Kingdom. God's love has been given to us by the Holy Spirit. This love, in turn, becomes the source from which Christian living flows.

We can easily overlook Paul's radical vision. After all, thinking of God in terms of love has been an incomplete Christian project. Christians have resorted to the image of God given throughout much of the Hebrew Scriptures, a God who loves us on the condition that we love God back. In this view, God's law and justice come before other attributes of God, at least in terms of emphasis. Love and mercy might be shown, but only after allegiance and behavior have proven something about our lives. If justice comes first, then the religious project has to be repairing the injustice by undergoing punishment. If love comes first, then the project basically involves restoring a broken relationship, one broken from our side but restored on God's side.

Moreover, if God's love is poured into our hearts, then God's grace—God's undeserved favor toward us—becomes the principle out of which we behave. Moral life is not fundamentally a strenuous exertion to fulfill a set of laws. Moral life, as difficult as it might well be at times, is more the expression of our relationship with the God of love reflected in our interior lives, our external behaviors, and our relationship with the cosmos. Even in Jewish life, what we call the Ten Commandments were

118

not primarily moral prescriptions so much as the terms on which the Jewish people based their common life of faith in God. Behavior was not "being good" but being a part of a people who had a relationship with God.

The Holy Spirit, God's love poured into our hearts, permits us to act from reconciliation, not from alienation. Christians live in a world charged with the presence and power of divine love, a power that, liberating them, gives them the capacity to liberate others through forgiveness and peace, and a power to live as a servant of others and creation.

In this view, good deeds are those that correspond to God's love and the relationship they imply; evil deeds, on the other hand, contradict and violate relationships of love. Good deeds are those that make the Kingdom more visible; evil deeds obscure or deform the Kingdom. Good deeds are those that further the purpose of creation, being part of that evolution of fullness we can identify as both believers and students of nature; evil deeds thwart creation's purpose, keeping it from proceeding toward that community of love God wills.

One filled with divine love does not obsess over sins and defects, honing a scrupulosity that obscures the nature of God. One filled with divine love concentrates on actions that look outward toward others in love and, therefore, serve to foster the possibilities that every person has so as to advance toward a greater fullness. Love, Paul reminds us, does not seek its own interest: "It bears all things, believes all things, hopes all things, endures all things" (1 Cor 13:7).

One of the questions that arose about the spiritual life was whether one could love God with complete selflessness. Could one, for example, love God so much that he or she prayed to be damned forever in order to eliminate eternal joy as a possibly selfish motive for loving God? The extreme of this question shows how convoluted our thinking can become. Would not a God of unbounded love want joy to be a splendid motive for our actions? Would a God of infinite love ever want the eternal damnation of anyone? The Kingdom is about the fullness of life and love received by creation insofar as that is possible. We humans, blessed as we are with consciousness and an unlimited horizon, have the capacity to receive this love with a unique depth.

Of course, humans must concern themselves with how they love. This concern, however, cannot void the reality that the Spirit of God has been given as God's commitment to us. God is not "yes" one minute and "no" another minute (2 Cor 1:18–20); God's commitment to us creates the possibility of our commitment to God and to others in God. Christian living rests on the faithfulness of God toward us; this faithfulness gives us the capacity to be faithful in giving ourselves in the image of God.

There is a *personal context* for our life of grace. Our inner mentality and our instinctual desires have to be shaped by our consciousness of divine love. Jesus's great amplifications of some of the assumptions of Jewish thinking ("You have heard from your fathers...") all revolve around shaping the inner instincts of our hearts. When talking about what makes someone unclean, Jesus does not point to any forbidden food; he points to attitudes that shape actions. "But what comes out of a person, that is what defiles. From within people, from their hearts, come evil thoughts, unchastity, theft, murder, adultery, greed, malice, deceit, licentiousness, envy, blasphemy, arrogance, folly. All these evils come from within and they defile" (Mark 7:20–23). This is very close to Paul's list of the works of "the flesh" in his letter to the

Galatians; pointedly, he tells his readers, "If we live in the Spirit, let us also follow the Spirit" (Gal 5:25). But there is no law against the gifts the Spirit bestows on us, gifts that shape an inner impulse to love: "The fruit of the Spirit is love, joy, peace, patience, kindness, generosity, faithfulness, gentleness, self-control" (Gal 5:22–23).

But our inner dispositions show themselves in our *social context* of our lives, because we all live in a highly connected set of relationships that, in fact, make up much of the life we experience. Every action toward others shapes their lives and actions. The assumptions and permission that we tolerate shape the common world in which we live. While we rightly think of our actions as primarily our own, they are, at the same time, the product of the world that has been given to us. Responsibility, therefore, cannot be only about our actions; it must be also about the moral environment that we shape and contribute to. No isolated circles of human life can be exempt from recognizing these connections, as if people on Wall Street or elegant Fifth Avenue were exempt from the circles of Main Street or the inner city. Collectively we construct the environment that, directly or indirectly, shapes what we think life is about. Christians, filled with the Spirit of divine love, live realizing their interconnectedness with the social world around them. Indeed, Christians may not control their environment, but we can always witness to the love we have found even if others cannot quite see it.

Our inner dispositions and our social actions inevitably connect with the *creation* that we are part of. Relationship extends far beyond and beneath our actions, whether personal or collective. Our human reality has resulted from relationships of matter and energy that extend back to what we call the Big Bang. The mysterious world of forces and particles, only incompletely unpacked, show the impact of everything on everything else. We cannot have an integral life without an integral society. But we cannot have an integral society without a world mostly undamaged and unpolluted. Sometimes it takes plagues or epidemics to show us how connected we ultimately are. But earth itself, the common land and water we share, demonstrates that connectedness as well. Noxious gasses do not stay in one state or one country. Exploitive use of fossil fuels does not impact one county or one community. The misuse of chemicals and nuclear energy do not stay with those who misuse; they spill over to everyone and everything. The effects of large weapons of destruction, almost by definition, intend a broad footprint. A worldview that focuses primarily on profit produces distorted intentions in every culture.

Can a way of life emerge for modern believers, one in which their positive orientation to the God of love helps them live focused on others, filled with the optimism that comes about when people understand life as a process of looking forward, of pushing ahead for something richer for everyone, of manifesting the abundant God of love more fully in daily life? A life rooted in the Spirit, dynamic and free, empowers believers to trust their hearts, to more frequently roll up their sleeves, to dare to cross the false boundaries we set up between each other, and to work for a view of life that ties everything together in relationship.

Can a life based on the Spirit help Christians understand more completely the purpose of Jesus's suffering? Can Christians acknowledge that the suffering of Jesus, real and catastrophic as it was, has been transcended in resurrection? Can we venerate Jesus on the cross in a way that lets us know we are sent forth from the cross in the power of the Spirit he breathes into us? Can living in the Spirit free us from the judgmental, scrupulous, fearful, avoidant attitudes that have come to haunt Christian spirituality so easily over the centuries?

Seeing

If we live in and for the Kingdom, can we see it?

The Book of Revelation, the last book in our Christian Bible, is a notoriously complicated set of images from a vein of writing that we call *apocalyptic*, a word that means something hidden is being revealed. This kind of speaking and thinking had a long pedigree in Jewish thinking, going back to prophets who used images to try to get their message across. The Book of Revelation, like much of this literature elsewhere, tries to give consolation and strength to people who are being persecuted and seek God's help. The successions of visions and imagery bring the book to a climax when "Babylon," which undoubtedly represented the occupiers of Israel, Rome, is crushed to destruction.

The book goes on to describe the following:

> I saw no temple in the city, for its temple is the Lord God almighty and the Lamb. The city had no need of sun or moon to shine on it, for the glory of God gave it light, and its lamp was the Lamb. The nations will walk by its light, and to it the kings of the earth will bring their treasure. During the day its gates will never be shut, and there will be no night there. (Rev 21:22–25)

Here we see an image that attempts to show human experience transformed. The central image is that of "city," not as a way to put down rural areas but as a way to talk about humankind gathered into a community. It describes how "the glory of God gave it light," very similar to the language we saw in Paul, when God will be "all in all" (1 Cor 15:31). The glory of God becomes the very light by which people see. So much will God's glory permeate everything that its presence will make everything shine.

The image continues into the next chapter:

> The throne of God and of the Lamb will be in it, and his servants will worship him. They will look upon his face, and his name will be on their foreheads. Night will be no more, nor will they need light from lamp or sun, for the Lord God shall give them light, and they shall reign forever and ever. (Rev 22:3–5)

These lines make clear that God will be immediately accessible to everyone, so much so that humans will need no light because "God shall give them light." The vision of God, when creation comes to fulfillment, will be seen both in God and in how God is reflected in and through creation, particularly in those created beings who have come to consciousness.

The whole idea of seeing God has competing traditions in Jewish thought. We can note some of those difficulties in the account of God speaking to Moses through the burning bush. Immediately we see how the writers have to use symbols to express the presence of God: Moses sees a bush that, although it is burning, is not consumed (Exod 3:2). When Moses comes near the burning bush, God speaks to him: "I am the God of your father, he continued, the God of Abraham, the God of Isaac, and the God of Jacob. Moses hid his face, for he was afraid to look at God" (Exod 3:6). The notion that people could not look at God receives exaggerated emphasis when, later on in the Book of Exodus, God would pass by Moses. God keeps Moses back until God passes by because Moses will not be allowed to see God's face, only God's back (see Exod 33:19ff.).

Nevertheless, in other places we hear that God spoke to Moses "face to face" as one speaks to one's friend (Exod 33:11). Earlier in the book, Moses takes a group of elders with him. They ascend a mountain where they see God and eat: "Moses then went up with Aaron, Nadab, Abihu, and seventy elders of Israel, and they beheld the God of Israel. Under his feet there appeared to be sapphire tilework, as clear as the sky itself. Yet he did not lay a hand on these chosen Israelites. They saw God, and they ate and drank" (Exod 24:9–11). This scene is so different in tone compared to some stories about Jacob in the Book of Genesis where he encounters God in a wrestling match (Gen 32:35). We also think of Abram who encounters the presence of God as if in a trance after offering sacrifices (Gen 15:9ff.).

Later on in Jewish experience, Isaiah has a vision of God during what must have been an experience of worship in the Temple. Isaiah's instinct is hardly to congratulate himself. "Then I said, 'Woe is me, I am doomed! For I am a man of unclean lips, living among a people of unclean lips, and my eyes have seen the King, the LORD of hosts!'" (Isa 6:5). Ezekiel has his own visions of the divine at the start of his book of prophecy. Vocabulary seems almost to fail him:

> Above the firmament over their heads was the
> likeness of a throne that looked like sapphire;

and upon this likeness of a throne was seated, up above, a figure that looked like a human being. And I saw something like polished metal, like the appearance of fire enclosed on all sides, from what looked like the waist up; and from what looked like the waist down, I saw something like the appearance of fire and brilliant light surrounding him. Just like the appearance of the rainbow in the clouds on a rainy day so was the appearance of brilliance that surrounded him. Such was the appearance of the likeness of the glory of the Lord. And when I saw it, I fell on my face and heard a voice speak. (Ezek 1:26–28)

Such is the appearance of "the likeness of the Lord," for if God transcends all created things, then one cannot "see" God in anything like ordinary human vision. God can appear only in some kind of likeness to make a representation on our retinas. Indeed, Jewish people would liken their appearance in the Temple as a seeing of God: Psalm 42 talks of "enter[ing] and see[ing] the face of God" (v. 3), and Psalm 11 says, "The Lord is in his holy temple; the Lord's throne is in heaven" (v. 4). Ezekiel has visions of God leaving the Temple during the time of exile in Babylon (580 BC) and likewise has visions of God returning to the Temple (cf. Ezek 10:18; 43:1–3).

All of these images were turned on their heads with the experience of Jesus Christ, who reveals God with an immediacy not encountered before. Look at the opening of the Letter to the Hebrews: "In times past, God spoke in partial and various ways to our ancestors through the prophets; in these last days, he spoke to us through a son, whom he made heir of all things and through whom he created the universe, who is the refulgence of his glory, the very imprint of his being, and who sustains all things by his mighty word" (Heb 1:1–3). Jesus, Christians believed, had brought a more direct revelation of God than ever before. In the Gospel of John, one of Jesus's disciples, Philip, asks him to show them the Father. Jesus seems astonished, saying, "Have I been with you for so long a time and you still do not know me, Philip? Whoever has seen me has seen the Father. How can you say, 'Show us the Father'?" (John 14:9). To see the face of Jesus, to experience his action, is, in effect, to see God.

Both John and Paul talk about seeing God or knowing God. The First Letter of John brings up the idea of seeing God: "Beloved, we are God's children now; what we shall be has not yet been revealed. We do know that when it is revealed we shall be like him, for we shall see him as he is" (1 John 3:2). John brings up the tension between the present moments in which we live and the fullness of life for which we long. But seeing God, when the fullness of revelation comes, will make us "like him," for we shall be able to see God "as he is." In other words, there is a reciprocal relationship between how we exist and how we are able to encounter God. In the same letter, John says, "No one has ever seen God. Yet, if we love one another, God remains in us, and his love is brought to perfection in us" (John 4:12). The vision of God becomes clear in the way we love each other. The fullness of life, when creation is complete, means loving each other with such a depth that God becomes visible through the love we have. Of course, our ability to love each other is itself a sign of God's action in our lives.

When Jesus talks to Nicodemus, that pious Pharisee who was curious about Jesus, they get into a discussion about how things happen, particularly when it comes to being "born again," or experiencing conversion. In his conversation Jesus talks about the subtle power of the Holy Spirit in our lives. Rather than dramatic outbursts or feelings that floor us, the Spirit's basic work is what the Spirit accomplishes in our lives, transforming our relationships, giving us the ability to live differently, and also the capacity to see God's action around and within us. Jesus says to Nicodemus, "The wind blows where it wills, and you can hear the sound it makes, but you do not know where it comes from or where it goes; so it is with everyone who is born of the Spirit" (John 3:8). We know the Spirit by what it brings about.

For Paul, to know God also involves a reciprocal process: we know God in proportion as we are known by God (Gal 4:9). The very process of refusing to hide from God, of exposing ourselves in our vulnerability to God, becomes the way in which God becomes known in our lives. Similarly, Paul asserts, that if someone knows God, that is because this person is known by God (1 Cor 8:3). The clarity we have of divine life comes as a result of opening ourselves to that love. As we let God shine in our hearts, so we come to know God through his Son, Jesus. "God who said, 'Let light shine out of darkness,' has shone in our hearts to bring to light the knowledge of the glory of God on the face of [Jesus] Christ" (2 Cor 4:6).

Meditation: The Spirit

Long ago I decided I liked being a Christian, someone interested in religion and faith, because the questions were never boring. Faith touches on depths and layers of reality that otherwise grow invisible. But once we pay attention to the dimensions of faith in our lives, then we begin to see everything relating to everything else.

And I grew to like that. Why should issues of God be separated from the worries I have about life? Why should striving for moral integrity not be connected to the divine love God pours into us? Can the dreams of universal peace be something apart from the way we see God relating to us?

I, like many Christians, can be a little cautious around language that concerns the Holy Spirit. Wow, I think, God is elusive enough, and now we have a Holy Spirit too! I've also experienced people who have expected me to have certain feelings and say specific things as if they were some kind of proof; if I don't have those feelings the way they do, they then conclude that I do not yet know the Holy Spirit.

But this can all be another form of separating things that really belong together, of finding distinctions and divisions that complicate our conversation and thinking. I fear somehow becoming like Joachim of Fiore, looking for the Spirit in an imagined new era while the Spirit is already abundantly present in the era in which we live.

Ultimately, I do not think I get very far by telling the Spirit how the Spirit should relate to me, to others, to the Church, or to the world. The unpredictable Spirit, as elusive as a breeze (John 3:8), in the end, speaks to us in the ways we can receive the Spirit. My task is not to predefine this but to watch the way the Spirit unites, transforms living, and deepens a vision inside me.

Jesus sends the Spirit to continue his mission of bringing about the Kingdom; the Spirit, therefore guides. We continue to ask for ongoing transformation in the Spirit's presence.

~ • ~

For Reflection and Discussion

Read the follow passage slowly.

John 14:7–14

"If you know me, then you will also know my Father. From now on you do know him and have seen him." Philip said to [Jesus], "Master, show us the Father, and that will be enough for us." Jesus said to him, "Have I been with you for so long a time and you still do not know me, Philip? Whoever has seen me has seen the Father. How can you say, 'Show us the Father'? Do you not believe that I am in the Father and the Father is in me? The words that I speak to you I do not speak on my own. The Father who dwells in me is doing his works. Believe me that I am in the Father and the Father is in me, or else, believe because of the works themselves. Amen, amen, I say to you, whoever believes in me will do the works that I do, and will do greater ones than these, because I am going to the Father. And whatever you ask in my name, I will do, so that the Father may be glorified in the Son. If you ask anything of me in my name, I will do it."

1. Which of the works of Jesus has revealed the Father most clearly to you?
2. What kind of connection can you make between the way we live and our ability to see God?
3. If someone asked you what you think heaven will be like, what would you say?

Slowly pray the Lord's Prayer and conclude by asking God's blessing on you and yours.

Chapter 9

___

LIVING FOR THE KINGDOM

There will be those who will say to you, "Look, there he is," [or] "Look, here he is." Do not go off, do not run in pursuit. For just as lightning flashes and lights up the sky from one side to the other, so will the Son of Man be [in his day].

(Luke 17:23-24)

I KNOW WHAT JESUS is talking about when he speaks of lightning. Sometimes in the summers we city dwellers would be sent, as children, to camp in the mountains north of New York City. All of it seemed strange to us, especially the sounds of insects in the night, notably the cicadas who produce something like a long-sustained shriek. We'd smell a skunk, wonder about bears, run from snakes, and flick caterpillars onto each other's backs.

But sometimes we'd be sitting around at evening time, picking up the first subtle change of wind, our skin responding to the cooler temperatures mingling with the humid air left over from the day. "Did you hear that?" Some of us didn't at first, but soon the rumbling of thunder seemed like artillery in battle. Then a rush of silence. Then something like a snap.

The whole sky seemed to light up from some of the brightest lightning we'd ever seen, so bright it turned

evening into a sudden dawn, so bright we saw our shad-
ows where they hadn't been two seconds before. Evening
was gone, but it wasn't daylight either. The twilight that
marks all human experience (if we were only aware of
it) suddenly revealed itself and overtook us no-longer-
cocky children from the big city. All we knew was that we
were enveloped in a light that came flashing as if out of
nowhere.

~ • ~

Perhaps no temptation has beset the followers of
Jesus more than doing just what he warned against, that
is, saying, "Look, there he is," or, "Here he is." The need
to feel that God is contained, located, fixed goes back
to Solomon's reflection that, although God transcends
the universe, God has nevertheless become accessible
through the Jewish Temple (1 Kgs 8:27–30). Of course,
in the saying quoted above, Jesus is not saying that the
Son of Man is nowhere; rather, he is pointing out that
the coming of the Son of Man always comes as a surprise.
Sure, we know that the lightning of Jesus's metaphor
comes from the very elements that created its possibility,
the meeting of two weather fronts. But when the Son of
Man comes, it always shocks us, like a bolt of lightning, a
surprise. The lightning reveals the energy already latent,
just as Jesus reveals God's immanent divine love.

Along with suddenness and shock, the Kingdom
comes with groaning that extends through all of creation.
Paul, in the remarkable eighth chapter of Romans, offers
this image:

I consider that the sufferings of this present
time are as nothing compared with the glory

to be revealed for us. For creation awaits with
eager expectation the revelation of the children
of God....We know that all creation is groaning
in labor pains even until now; and not only that,
but we ourselves, who have the firstfruits of the
Spirit, we also groan within ourselves as we
wait for adoption, the redemption of our bodies.
(Rom 8:18–19, 22–23)

Rather than explosive lightning, we have the image of
long-term groaning, a cry that emerges in us who give
voice to the groaning built into creation itself. Instead of
lightning, Paul invites us to see a woman giving birth,
the process essential to human existence itself. Creation
groans, indeed, but it also longs, as a woman longs for her
child to appear. Creation lives in suspense, wondering
what will come about, dreaming of the new life that shows
itself in patient growth as well as the pangs of childbirth.
Paul is saying that creation itself lives in a restless desire
until the children of God are revealed, that is to say, until
those who have recognized and lived in relationship with
God can be shown as the crowning achievement of creation itself. Followers of Jesus, who have come to live for
the Kingdom of God, thrive by knowing that, adopted as
daughters and sons, they are made part of the victory of
Christ. They are part of his resurrection, which was that
moment when creation explicitly began to experience the
fulfillment latent within it.

Virtues

The followers of Jesus give birth, on behalf of creation,
to a future that appears as ever new and ever surprising.

This happens through the virtues that the Holy Spirit, Easter's greatest gift, bestows on those who come to faith. To live for the Kingdom means living in obedience to the gifts the Spirit pours into our lives, not for our own sakes but for the sake of all, for the sake of creation itself.

The gift of the virtue of love, God's love given and living in us, teaches us just this. For how long has love been conceived of as the fulfillment of desperate longing? For how long has love been enslaved to desire? Of course, sometimes the noblest desires produce art, literature, and culture. But, at the same time, do not the most self-centered desires often lead us to grab, possess, and even stifle? Does not history describe in wretched detail the cost of this self-centered love, from the destruction of earth and its resources to the exploitation of humans, even to the point of slavery and death?

Yet the love of the Holy Spirit leads elsewhere because it gives us a share in God's love, which provides a powerful alternative to self-centered love. For the love of God liberates the beloved, affirms the beloved, gives life to the beloved, and, pointedly, leads the beloved to selflessly love others. Of course, our very state as finite people drives us to get what we need to live. But onto this finite state of need and desire, now sanctified by the death and resurrection of Jesus, God has woven another pattern of love, one that principally asks not what we need to live but, more, what we have that we can give. However much humankind needs the erotic dimension of its existence, it also needs to transform this desire-driven human dimension into a quest to give ourselves in love to others, especially those most overlooked and forgotten.

In a curious way, the other-directed quality of love brings into human consciousness the other-directed quality of evolutionary creation itself. From this perspective, everything comes into being for another as life takes advantage of life to forge ahead into greater complexity; this complexity becomes, in turn, the basis of the emergence of intelligence and also of organizational relationships that intelligence generates, such as government and its favored model, the city. The drive of nature toward this complexity, from which relationship becomes possible, arises, in the eyes of a believer, from the other-directed love of God whose being pulls creation forward toward the fullness of reflecting God's life in its finite structures.

The dynamic of love accompanies yet another gift of the Holy Spirit: faith, which is the initial vision of the Kingdom of God as revealed through God's interactions with humankind through Jesus and the Spirit. Faith is itself an anticipation. Many naively use the phrase "blind leap of faith," as if faith had no basis but human wishing. But the keenest observers of belief see faith as the initial vision of something greater than everyday human experience, the vision of a level of reality that, while transcending everything else, relates everything else to itself. Believers have the ability to see everything coordinated with the God of unbounded love. From its initial and inchoate glimpses, faith builds a vision that comes ultimately as a gift. While faith may well come as a surprise (think of Paul struck to the ground in Acts 9:1ff.), it comes more as an exhilarating completion of something formerly only hinted, only sensed, indeed, only wished for.

Think of how things dawn on us. It's a different mental process than learning something or using information that we have, activities I might do while working on a budget or studying for an exam. But knowledge through things dawning on us works very differently. While based on the information we have picked up, it comes as a surprise as we see deeper, formerly unseen, connections. And it comes as a gift, as the fruit of a mind able to coordinate more fully and see more deeply. Faith works at this level, not as the conclusion of an argument, but as the surprising insight into the nature of creation and the nature of God. "Now I see why I expect good and truth, why evil and deceit upset me!" Faith is the dawning on us that comes in the form of an encounter with a God whose love seems, alone, to explain our lives.

The Letter to the Hebrews relates faith to hope: "Faith is the realization of what is hoped for and evidence of things not seen" (Heb 11:1). Just as love and faith relate to each other, so these both relate profoundly to hope. Hope provides the vision of a fullness toward which faith and hope direct themselves. Hope induces believers to hold their heads high as creation moves toward completion (Luke 21:28). Even in the face of what seem like catastrophes and certain destruction, believers know that God has already directed creation toward a path of victory in the resurrection of Jesus from the dead, the firstfruits of creation's fulfillment. Hope's vision looms greater yet than any prospect of doom or cowering in despair. Before the temptation to get stuck at one or another point in our lives, hope hurls believers forward toward horizons beyond any sticking points in human life.

Surely every epoch of Christian life has been marked by hope because the image of the Kingdom has made an indelible stamp on Christian faith. But, paradoxically, an unintegrated grasp of the Kingdom could often bring Christians to despise the world given to us rather than cherish that world as the environment from which the Kingdom is emerging. This kind of far-off hope created the "pie in the sky" vision of heaven that Karl

Marx famously mocked. Instead of parsing our moments in present life, we longed for a world elsewhere, describing present existence as mostly "a valley of tears." As such, the misery, lowliness, finiteness, and limitations that beset human experience had to be endured for the sake of a Kingdom that would come as a prize after our earth was destroyed. If this was the vision of Jesus, what was his healing and feeding people about? Why would he have proclaimed people blessed and happy? Why would he rise from the dead with the very body scarred by his political execution?

One way of seeing the list of virtues that emerged in the Middle Ages was to think of them as "habits," not in the sense of mindless repetitive actions but in the sense of dispositions poised toward certain good actions. We might imagine the way an athlete's training would dispose her to hit a tennis ball in a certain way that benefitted her game. Or how the long studies of a student led her to be proficient in law. In other words, potentials for good would, with training, tend to become actualities.

In this way, the virtues of faith, hope, and love—the primary gifts of the Holy Spirit in our lives—become a way by which our actions are shaped a certain way. And those actions become part of the universe of actions that lead the potentiality of creation toward greater completion. This is what the faithful have seen in their saints: people whose lives have been disposed to show the qualities of God's love and life through their own acts. While we admire the heroic actions of saints like Paul, Francis Xavier, and Teresa of Avila, some of the most memorable saints in recent centuries have emphasized that it is in the "little deeds" we do that God's love radiates most regularly in our lives. St. Thérèse of Lisieux, for example, taught her "little way," which held that every little deed we do, done in love, shows the glory of God. St. Teresa of Calcutta reminded the world that people in need are all around us; we don't have to go to India to show care for others. When we attend to the present with the powers that virtues bring us, we slowly open the future God wills for us.

We can, in this way, conceive all of moral life as an exercise of virtues, an exercise of bringing the potential goodness of human actions into reality. Just as we can examine our moral lives as to whether they correspond to the Kingdom or not, so also we can examine ourselves in terms of the virtues that have been cultivated in our lives as well as the vices that have hampered our life of virtue. The virtues of faith, hope, and love, after all, are all dimensions of living in the Kingdom of God. Developing these virtues in our lives would line up with some of the most solid moral thinking in the history of the Church.

Sacrament

Christian life comes as a gift of the Holy Spirit who actualizes our human potential in the direction of Christ's Kingdom. Christians experience this life on many levels, but the most explicit experience of the Spirit's work is through the worship of the Church through actions we call sacraments. The word itself indicates a revealing of something deeper, the making clear of something that is hidden or implicit. We can think of sacraments as those sacred actions of celebration by the Church that bring about a new relationship with God and others, or that reveal a relationship that has already begun. Sacraments are sacred points on a continuum of experience.

Christians enter the Kingdom in an explicit way when they receive the sacrament of baptism, which celebrates and signifies a life with God that has already begun even before the sacrament is received. Baptism clearly shows us that the Kingdom is not some aloof realm that is a reward for doing good; no, the Kingdom is the life already begun by the community of Christ's followers. The Church has considered catechumens, adults preparing for baptism, to already be members of the Church before receiving the sacrament. And parents can bring their infants to be baptized because the child has already been situated in an environment of faith. Parents communicate a vision of God, salvation, and life from the first moments of contact with their baby; indeed, this vision is implicit in the very love parents show each other before the child is even conceived. Water, the natural element used in baptism, shows that this sacrament is available to anyone who can thirst and drink.

Baptism does far more than prepare us for a future life beyond death. It makes us members of a community of faith whose very nature is to serve the world by its vision of faith and life. Baptism brings us into a Church whose community is itself structured by the Holy Spirit, the Spirit of divine love. The Church is not some accident in history. The Church is history preparing for the birth of the fullness of the Kingdom. Just as no person lives exclusively for him- or herself, so the Church does not live for itself (even though that may seem to be the case for large periods of its history). The Church lives for the world—as its sacrament and its servant. Baptism brings us into a community that speaks the language of the Kingdom, fosters the actions of the Kingdom, and signifies the breadth of the Kingdom in its prayer and worship. We note in the baptism ceremony how the believer has been moved from the "kingdom of darkness" into the "kingdom of light." Once we are baptized, on one or another level of consciousness, we begin living for the Kingdom in a community defined by it.

Baptism commissions believers to serve the world in such a way that all the dimensions of life are cherished and served. Through baptism the Holy Spirit empowers believers to be instruments through which the world is led to a more compassionate future.

Does not Eucharist show us what this community is about? Does not Eucharist gather us as sisters and brothers, privilege us to hear the Word of God, and then bring us to that very point in which Christ transcended the limits of death as he opened up human life to God's own life? The Eucharist is where we are made spiritually one—with Christ in his endless praise of the Father, in his endless revealing of the Father's love, and in his endless gift of the Holy Spirit to humankind.

If creation, evolving from its first nanoseconds, culminates in the person of Jesus who brings creation into the fullness of God's life, believers, joined in Eucharist, consciously become one with this dynamic force that shapes life and history. Indeed, Eucharist brings believers to a timeless point within time, where the layers of existence compress themselves through the act of worship. Earth itself strains forth in the Eucharist, touching the contours of eternity, and divine life pushes forth, transforming the contours of time.

Eucharist, indeed, means union with Jesus through holy communion. But its whole context says it means yet more than this. Eucharist is the highest instance of creation consciously acknowledging the fullness of God in and through human experience. The Book of Revelation often conceives of eternal life as worshipful chants of the saved rejoicing in God. The Eucharist shows us that those chants, if they will be fully sung, have their beginning when believers gather as a living sacrament to thank God through the Eucharist.

Pope Francis alludes to this in paragraph 236 of his encyclical on the environment, *Laudato Si'*:

> It is in the Eucharist that all that has been created finds its greatest exaltation. Grace, which tends to manifest itself tangibly, found unsurpassable expression when God himself became man and gave himself as food for his creatures. The Lord, in the culmination of the mystery of the Incarnation, chose to reach our intimate depths through a fragment of matter. He comes not from above, but from within, he comes that we might find him in this world of ours. In the Eucharist, fullness is already achieved; it is the living center of the universe, the overflowing core of love and of inexhaustible life.

In Eucharist believers see creation expressing its highest dignity: to acknowledge the endless love and generosity through thanksgiving. Time and space, matter and spirit, flesh and heart, nature and craft—they all come together in the unity that Christians celebrate around the table of the Lord. As Jesus once took on our flesh, he continues to take on the flesh of all those united with him as part of the continuation of his mission. To dare to receive his Body is to plead, at the same time, to become his Body in the world. As his risen Body shows our future, so our sharing in his risen Body continues to open this future to human experience.

So often our ideas of the Eucharist turn us backward in time, toward Jesus's death and toward ancient images of sacrifice. But how much of the Eucharist actually pushes us forward, toward the fulfillment of creation and the heavenly banquet that was one of Jesus's basic images in his ministry? When we gather in Eucharist, Jesus gives us the ability to dare to embody the final state of our completion.

Yet we gather in Eucharist as a community that has experienced mercy and, therefore, the possibility of reconciliation. Mercy means that God's healing love is bringing creation back to its ultimate purpose, back toward the goal of the Kingdom. When mercy is accepted, God's forgiveness moves us into a new realm of experience, one in which brokenness finds healing, division dissolves into unity, estrangement discovers oneness. Mercy is God's loving initiative toward broken humankind; God's selfless love, through mercy, begins to neutralize the self-centered love that cripples human experience. To celebrate the sacrament of reconciliation means rejoicing in the healing that God has brought into our lives and, for that reason, into the world.

Healing, as we saw, was one of Jesus's most pronounced actions. The first time he sends his disciples out in ministry it is to do deeds of healing (Mark 6:7–13), whether of peoples' bodies or their spirits. For what traps us, limits us, or isolates us more than illness? We think of the paralyzed people, crippled, blind, and deaf people whom Jesus touched. In every case it was to restore those people to their communities and to show them as instances of the healing that every person needs. When creation comes to its fullness, every human will be able to participate if she or he has been healed in some way. Was not the resurrection of Jesus the healing of the wounds that he bore on the part of all of us?

The Church celebrates healing through laying on of hands and anointing with oil. Imposing hands on the sick person represents the sharing of the Spirit of healing that God has given to believers; the gulf between sufferer and healer is bridged. Anointing the sick person with oil represents the soothing embrace that accompanies every desire for healing. Bridging the gulfs between us, offering embraces that console, being a Church freely offering the healing that God extends to all: is this not the calling of every parish, of every community of faith? And is not every believer in Jesus called to extend healing to others as much as possible?

Indeed, one of the essential processes of creation is also revealed as sacred in the sacrament of matrimony. For human sexuality surely is part of that groaning of all creation that Paul was talking about in Romans 8. Life pushes to beget new life. Life insists that our genes need to be completed by the genes of another. Life expresses its dynamic interconnectedness in the begetting and rearing of every child. Life says this precious begetting of people needs the faithful care of partners who commit themselves completely to each other. Because humans might produce children apart from total commitment, when their sexual expression involves more a using of another than a giving oneself to another, the child who is born often must bear testimony to what was needed and what was lacking by having to live a more conflicted life. That the Church insists that love be unconditional, exclusive, faithfully enduring, and open to life shows just how well it has read the human heart and the ultimate destiny of creation, as well as the love God shows us. Couples who love faithfully sacramentalize for us the

143

other-directed love of God that is the origin and the goal of creation itself. Their love creates, as it were, the ideal world in the scale of their lives.

Living for the Kingdom involves, as well, people being willing to commit themselves to be clear witnesses to the place of the Kingdom in human life. The sacrament of holy orders, which establishes roles by which believers live to give testimony to the Kingdom through presiding over sacred actions, really is an intensification of the sacraments of baptism and confirmation, the sacraments in which discipleship is accepted and affirmed. Christ gives priesthood to the whole Church, for every believer has the charge of dedicating the world to God's vision; deacons, priests, and bishops make this priesthood explicit by the ways of life they involve, all of them for the sake of building up the Church (and not oneself).

One of the classic ways of describing sacraments was through the formula of "matter and form," in which bread or water would constitute the matter, and the prayers and intentions would constitute the form. We can apply an evolutionary viewpoint to this ancient approach: sacraments show how the matter of creation, the material world, becomes transformed and elevated to accomplish the sacred purposes of God. Every sacrament is a sign of the Kingdom and a step within it. Every sacrament "confers grace," as we used to put it, because it situates us more clearly in one or another dimension of the Kingdom into which believers have entered through their participation in the Church. Through belonging and commitment, through mercy and healing, through states of selfless giving, Christians show the Kingdom being lived out in this phase of time.

But we call these actions sacraments precisely because they point beyond themselves into a vast vision that constitutes the ultimate way to interpret human life and experience.

Meditation: Externals

Perhaps I think my faith is all implicit, hidden behind rites, practices, and memorized lines from the Catechism or some other book. Perhaps I feel my faith is mostly external, a cultural accretion I've not been able to shake.

Can I unpack the formulas, the rituals, the external practices? Can I find the commitments in my life that lie behind them?

Because faith is a constant part of my life—not just when I'm connected to Church but mostly when I'm engaged with others, the sense of God buried deeply within me comes across when I speak to others, when I offer my services, when I spontaneously pray, when I reach out to another.

When I do something, my community of faith is somehow also present. For where did I learn about faith, celebrate faith, reflect on faith, and commit myself to believe? Didn't I do this when I went to Mass last Sunday and heard the Gospel read? Didn't I do this when I joined others in the congregation to affirm Jesus as our eternal priest? Didn't I do this when I went forth to receive holy communion and reached for the consecrated bread saying, "Amen"?

When I wanted to give up and throw in the towel, what kept me from doing that? When I wanted to wallow in self-pity and enjoy being immobilized by my tears, what pulled me from my slump? When I was asked to do something I really did not want to do, but I did it anyway because someone needed me, what gave me the power?

If I think perhaps my faith is all external, maybe I have to think more deeply, observe more fully, and accept more readily. "The Spirit of God is upon me," as the hymn goes.

I know that, of course. I need to remember that more.

~ • ~

For Reflection and Discussion

Read the following passage slowly.

Galatians 5:19–26

Now the works of the flesh are obvious: immorality, impurity, licentiousness, idolatry, sorcery, hatreds, rivalry, jealousy, outbursts of fury, acts of selfishness, dissensions, factions, occasions of envy, drinking bouts, orgies, and the like. I warn you, as I warned you before, that those who do such things will not inherit the kingdom of God. In contrast, the fruit of the Spirit is love, joy, peace, patience, kindness, generosity, faithfulness, gentleness, self-control. Against such there is no law. Now those who belong to Christ [Jesus] have crucified their flesh with its passions and desires. If we live in the Spirit, let us also follow the Spirit. Let us not be conceited, provoking one another, envious of one another.

1. What do you think of the list of virtues that Paul attributes to the Holy Spirit? Think about the context in which they might be lived.
2. Look at the list of vices that Paul considers works of the flesh. How many of them are personal? How many are social? How do we tend to think about vices today?

3. From this passage, what do you think Paul saw as the most essential element of living for the Kingdom? What was the greatest sign that one was living for the Kingdom?

Slowly pray the Lord's Prayer and conclude by asking God's blessing on you and yours.

Chapter 10

CONCLUSION

A Spirituality of the Kingdom

IF A SPIRITUALITY INVOLVES assumptions, attitudes, and behaviors, what might these be for a spirituality of discipleship in the Kingdom?

A disciple has her heart fixed on the Kingdom, both its promise and its present reality. Everything in his experience relates, in some way, to the vision of Jesus. What drove Jesus's life comes to drive our lives as well.

A disciple sees himself as a living witness, called to bear testimony about what God is doing in the world. Living as a witness means putting the message of good news before anything else in her life. As Jesus lived his witness without thought of the cost to himself, so disciples do not add up the costs of following Jesus. They live only to magnify the Father through their words and deeds.

Likewise, a disciple sees creation and experience as one unbroken vision. Because everything is linked and related, the earliest potential of the Big Bang (or however one might construe the origins of the cosmos) stands connected to the final fulfillment of the Kingdom. The purpose of creation, then, is exactly to bring about the Kingdom that Jesus inaugurates.

A disciple sees selfless love as the fundamental élan of the world in which he lives. Because evolution shows a creation of processes in which all its elements find their meaning in the other, so divine love is more fully reflected in those who find fulfillment in serving others. The pre-mind processes of evolution find their consciousness in the emergence of human life with its capacity to know and love.

A disciple living for the Kingdom sees her life pitched forward toward what will come to be. The elements of life receive their sacredness not only from their origin in the divine but, even more, in their capacity to stretch forward into the future, to live for an end that is divine as well.

Discipleship in the Kingdom calls for interpreting experience integrally. This kind of vision resists categorizing experience into dimensions that seem separate from, if not hostile to, each other. Matter is not against spirit; this life is not against the next life; nature is not inimical to supernature; time does not fight with eternity.

A disciple in the Kingdom interprets experience in terms of relationship (even more than being); the purpose of being is to be in relationship, primarily with God, but just as fundamentally with the world and, most particularly, with the complex of relationships involved in life.

Relationship achieves a distinct fullness with the experience of joy, that sense of being freed because of the abundance of divine love and the ability to sustain relationships with others through God's love. True joy (far more than transactional pleasure) is the unfailing sign of the presence of the Kingdom.

A spirituality of the Kingdom strives for more than awareness or even inner perfection. The Kingdom consists of people coming to relate to each other in the model of God's self-giving love. Connections with others, and actions that flow from those connections, make up the central matter of the spiritual life. Kingdom attitudes flow into Kingdom behaviors; unless they do, the attitudes are self-posturing and empty.

A disciple in the Kingdom understands the gravity of sin as those actions that stand counter to the emergence of the Kingdom. Sins are those deeds that—unwilling to break beyond self-centeredness—disrupt, disvalue, and dissolve the relationships essential for the fullness of creation. The separation between sin and the Kingdom can only be overcome by a transformation that allows one to see, and live for, the Kingdom once again. Mercy and reconciliation are the divine initiatives by which this separation is conquered.

Creation becomes a process of reconciliation once sin "enters the world," to use Paul's phrase (Rom 5:12). But the narration at the start of the Jewish and Christian Bibles about the first couple reveals a constant option always present for humans, one that has defined all human existence. This option toward negation of the Kingdom shows the need for reconciliation, which happens in the death and resurrection of Jesus Christ.

A disciple living for the Kingdom sees Jesus's death in more than "justice" terms in which an angry God demands justice for offenses committed. Rather, Jesus's death is itself reconciliation, both creating a situation in which humankind and God can relate to each other without estrangement once again, and also revealing the scope of the Kingdom as transcending the limit of human death. Whereas estrangement begins with humankind, reconciliation begins with the God who offers, in his Son Jesus, recourse for humans to live in and for the Kingdom once again. Jesus's life and death look forward, not just backward.

Conclusion

Disciples incarnate in themselves the paschal mystery, which Jesus gave us as a model for human existence. In letting go, in giving himself, in submitting to death, Jesus shows us the way to true life and resurrection. The pattern of death and resurrection reigns in the heart of every disciple as death to self-centeredness and life for self-gift.

Discipleship in the Kingdom means being free by the gift of the Holy Spirit who bestows on us the powers and virtues by which we can direct our lives to the fullness God proposes for us. The Spirit provides the dynamic energy that restores relationships with creation and with others.

A disciple for the Kingdom venerates the sacramental role the Church has to play in God's vision, to be the herald of a worldwide community of love, grace, peace-seeking, healing, and transformation. The breadth of the Kingdom can be grasped only in a living community that, for all its potential flaws, still serves a divine role as God's harbinger of fulfillment.

A disciple in the Kingdom sees his Church as a sacrament of the Kingdom, a sign of what God would do for all of humankind. For this reason, a disciple expects his Church to relate to others in love and respect. Because of the sweep of the Kingdom in and through the Church, the Church does not have to define itself in exclusive terms. Rather, it relates to all with whom it can relate, and it seeks to include all that can be included. As a result, disciples find joy in dialogue with other believers, confident that the Spirit will bring to maturity its inner workings in every human heart.

To be a disciple means cultivating a conscious, personal relationship with God as revealed in his Son Jesus and in the dynamics of the Holy Spirit. Such a personal relationship necessitates the recourse to the Holy Scriptures, which provide the images and language needed to have access to God. Recourse to the Holy Scriptures and growth in prayer entail an ongoing conversion, an ongoing transformation of mind and heart so the contours of the Kingdom can be more clearly seen and obeyed.

To a disciple, the sacred actions of the Church, particularly its sacraments, reveal and grant more fully access to the unending dynamic of God's transforming love. Disciples see the sacraments as pointers to the concrete reality of the Kingdom. The forms and gestures of the sacraments, made from the elements of the earth and from the most fundamental of human gestures, continue the earthly, human reality of Jesus, God's Son made flesh. Water, oil, bread; gestures of consoling and reconciling; acts of abiding commitment to love selflessly—these form the basics of sacramental experience, all of them seeking to implement the Kingdom.

Disciples also see sacraments as pushing humankind forward toward the Kingdom. The washing of baptism represents the taking on of a new life in the Kingdom; the unity of the Eucharist represents the Sacred Banquet that is the ultimate metaphor of the Kingdom; the capacity to ask for and receive forgiveness shows the endless possibilities of mercy in the Kingdom; the embrace of marriage is the love-filled embrace of a future that cannot be predicted but still compels; ordination means accepting the responsibility to make the signs of the Kingdom into a totally committed way of life; anointing with oil shows the renewal that the hope of healing offers everyone. Every sacrament receives its deepest meaning with reference to a Kingdom constantly being born and constantly shaping history.

To be a disciple is to be committed to serving whatever brings about a more authentic wholeness of humankind and for creation. Disciples are willing to stand on the horizon, looking forward to a future for which existence longs, pioneers of a vision crucial for human life itself. Standing on the horizon means standing for the most broken and neglected because they need a vision of a future more fundamentally than the comfortable do. The horizon calls us to bring news of joy and hope to the poor, to find ways to liberate the trapped and addicted, to give vision and direction to those who cannot see and will not hear, and to be living signs of the transformation that beckons.

~ • ~

A basic vision for future discipleship was laid out in the encyclical *Laudato Si'* in a paragraph near the end. It offers an outline for religious thinking as we enter the future.

The divine Persons are subsistent relations, and the world, created according to the divine model, is a web of relationships. Creatures tend towards God, and in turn it is proper to every living being to tend towards other things, so that throughout the universe we can find any number of constant and secretly interwoven relationships. This leads us not only to marvel at the manifold connections existing among creatures, but also to discover a key to our own fulfilment. The human person grows more, matures more and is sanctified more to the extent that he or she enters into relationships, going out from themselves to live in communion with God, with others and with all creatures. In this way, they make their own that trinitarian dynamism which God imprinted in them when they were created. Everything is interconnected, and this invites us to develop a spirituality of that global solidarity which flows from the mystery of the Trinity. (no. 240)

In this telling, to have come to appropriate the trinitarian dynamism in our lives and in history is to, finally, fully attain the Kingdom of God.

Meditation: Here I Am

Perhaps the very simplicity of the melody and the words make the hymn all the more gripping. It isn't sung all that often in churches; when it is, singers might miss a note or two. But when it is sung, uniformly and with energy, hardly any other piece seems as haunting.

"Here I am, Lord; here I am, I come to do your will." Rory Cooney's version of Psalm 40, which the Letter to the Hebrews uses to organize one of its major points (Heb 10:7), transposed the psalm's ideas into very direct ideas: "It was you who taught my heart to sing, to sing a song of joy."

It was my second visit to a parish near Dayton, Ohio; I had once again presented ideas about forming small groups and discipleship. The pastor invited me to celebrate the Saturday evening Mass. To my surprise, people filled the church. The cantor was a teen or a very young adult who had a great sense of herself and her role. As the

Conclusion

music began and I realized I would be hearing one of my favorite modern hymns, I looked at the cantor.

It wasn't just the force of her voice; it was the way she looked around at the congregation as she sang, as if deliberately calling them to attention. She sang the opening verse and then raised her hand, the sign that the congregation would begin singing. They echoed the force and conviction of the cantor's voice. The congregation, almost as a single person, filled the building with their swelling voices: "Here I am, Lord; here I am. I come to do your will."

I have thought of this event many times, especially as ideas of Catholic discipleship are bandied about. While it is so easy to rank Catholics fairly low on the discipleship scale (don't know the Bible, don't read the Bible, don't share faith, don't reach out to others, etc.), I keep pondering what I witnessed: a congregation of over eight hundred people singing their hearts out about doing the will of God, the very same desire that fixed Jesus's attention.

Certainly we need to be committed to calling believers to a more overt and powerful discipleship; indeed, even for the most fervent and active of our parishioners this is true. But do we discount what the Spirit accomplishes in believers as a normal part of their faith lives too readily? The spontaneous prayers, the celebrating of sacraments, the religious formation they receive? Their desire to do what is right, to roll up sleeves, to go out of their way to make someone else's life a little better? The way hymns with profound meaning and commitment surge from their voices, whether accompanied by organ or by guitar? "Holy God we praise thy name." "And I will raise you up!" The sense of themselves now more clearly infused with a knowledge of God's love for them and for all people? Do we overlook these and other signs too easily?

155

DISCIPLESHIP FOR THE FUTURE

Not long after this sung testimony of faith and commitment, I went to the pulpit to read the Gospel and preach. It was John's account of the disciples' earliest following of Jesus. "Where do you live?" they asked Jesus. "Come and see," he said.

Whatever I had to say to this congregation who had invited me there to advance the cause of discipleship, I could not actually match what the congregation had said to me. I had witnessed the powerful echo of their faith, the song of disciples yearning to share in the Kingdom.

Behind our somewhat creaky structures; through the patterns we have set up for worship, education, and community; aside from all the problems an ancient Church faces in a world that changes dramatically by the generation, there I clearly heard it. A note had sounded. A song had begun. A community of parishioners had taken the theme—I come to do your will—and made it their own, a theme that showed how eager they were to embrace the future God was opening for them.

156